what's going on?

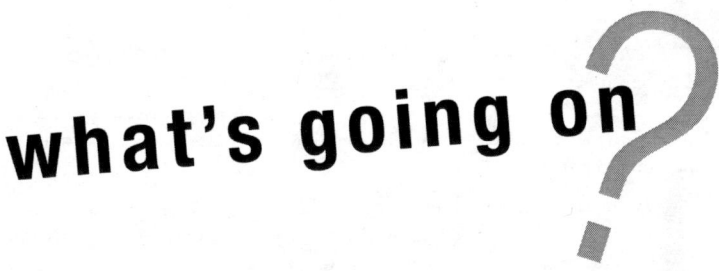

what's going on?

THE EMERGING TROUBLE ON THE HORIZON

KENNETH HOFFMAN

TATE PUBLISHING & Enterprises

Published by Tate Publishing & Enterprises, LLC
127 E. Trade Center Terrace | Mustang, Oklahoma 73064 USA
1.888.361.9473 | www.tatepublishing.com

Tate Publishing is committed to excellence in the publishing industry. The company reflects the philosophy established by the founders, based on Psalm 68:11,
"The Lord gave the word and great was the company of those who published it."

Book design copyright © 2008 by Tate Publishing, LLC. All rights reserved.
Cover design by Lynly Taylor
Interior design by Isaiah R. McKee

Published in the United States of America

ISBN: 978-1-60604-282-3
1. Current Events: History: Analysis 2. Future

08.05.20

The events that took place before the 2nd World War are taking place at this very moment. The U.S.A. and the rest of the world were trying to ignore what was happening. Burying their head in the sand and make believe that if they ignore what is taking place. Every thing will be alright.

What is happening in the World as seen through the eyes of someone born in 1935.

Kenneth Hoffman

What's going on?

The emerging trouble on the horizon is how American politics contribute to the problem. We cannot make believe that what is happening isn't real. We must deal with the truth.

If you are a Christian, go to John 8:32 which reads, "And ye shall know the truth and the truth will make you free."

If you are not a Christian you still must know the truth, before you can deal with an issue/problem. If you do not know the truth you cannot free yourself-solve the problem.

Kenneth Hoffman

Dedication

Let freedom ring
To the melding pot of the world and greatest
people on earth
The American people

Acknowledgements

This book was inspired by visiting with many people over about a two year time line. Talking to about 300 to 400 people about our great country and what has taken place in their life time. To those who contributed to this effort with their frank answers, to my many probing questions, I want to say thank you from the bottom of my heart. Without your answers this endeavor would not have taken place. Again thank you for your encouragement, when I told you the purpose of my probing.

This has been a real challenge for me. Without the Chronicle of the 20th century book it would have been a real challenge, to find the dates and events of the 1st World War, the roaring 20's, the Great Depression, and the 2nd World War. This allowed me to do the overview of all of these events in order without too much effort. Thank you from the bottom of my heart.

I would like to thank my son Kirk R. Hoffman. For taking time to read the rough draft of: *What's Going On?* Expressing his views about what he garnered from it. For writing the Foreword to the book, Kirk, thank you for your time and effort. Good job!

I know that many of the people that contributed to *what's going on* do not even know that they were contributors. I would like to offer a thank you, to them in absentia. When they read the book many of them will recognize, why I was probing them with questions about our great country.

I would like to thank my friends in Indiana for e-mailing me the Reagan, Roosevelt quotes, and the cartoon about the oil shortage.

I would like to thank my wife for putting up with me, serving me coffee and keeping our dogs busy so they would not bother me.

Kenneth Hoffman
Theodosia, Missouri
October 2007

Foreword

While reading: *What's Going On* I received a powerful message about what is happening in the world and this great country of ours. And how what is being said about the events that are taking place affect the U.S.A. How our politicians are mishandling the situation by not presenting a united front to the world. The message is "united we stand, divided we fall." Kenneth Hoffman points out, get it together soon. Time is running out. I believe he is right. The message about our leaders, wasting most of their time bickering, debating and not showing up for work 50% of the time and doing strange things in bathrooms, pleading guilty, procrastinating. Plus many other unethical actions, is right on track. Kenneth Hoffman does not pick on Democrats or Republicans. But instead is unbiased in his pursuit of change for the better.

Kenneth Hoffman in: *What's Going On* Chronicles highlights of the events of the 1st World War, the start of the industrial revolution, the roaring 20's and the Great Depression. How Hitler and Japan brought us to the brink. Many of the great leaders of that era and beyond are touted by Kenneth Hoffman. Being of the caliber we need today; He states we have not had a good leader since Ronald Reagan or Jack Kennedy was President. I believe he is correct in saying so. His message is powerful he asks our leaders "are you truly honest?" Then he gives them a standard by which to self-evaluate, so they can see for themselves if they measure up. He asks them to sit down in front of a mirror. Ask them selves if they were ever guilty of attaching an earmark-pork project to an important bill so they could bleed the resources of our nation for their own use. Kenneth Hoffman states that we people can only go by what we see happening. It is not good he believes that you are part of the problem or part of the solution. He says if you are using your office that we placed you in, to power broker events for your own benefit then you need to change your ways.

He believes that we need to get back to the Christian principles that this nation was founded on. He believes that they are sound, moral and ethical ways to live by. He also asks us to teach our children the 10 commandments. He states if our children were taught to live by them. We would not have the problems we have today.

He does not believe there should be any preferential treatment of any American regardless of where they come from or their background. So long as they are Americans. He states we must all be Americans first if we live in America. We all must speak English. We are an English speaking nation. All of our schools teach English as the primary language. It is up to a student if they want to learn a second language. He states it must be that way. He also believes that a student take a second language it builds character.

I feel: What's Going On is a must read for all Americans. It has a message for liberal, conservative and independent alike. It is not biased to any group of people. Kenneth Hoffman feels he expounds on the beliefs of most Americans. We must remember that the approval rating for our Congress is at 18% at this moment, which means the American public knows you are doing a poor job, at best. He also has done a limited poll and found the approval rating to be 5%.

Kirk R. Hoffman

I was born September 6th, 1935 to American parents of German blood. My great grandparents immigrated to the U.S.A. in the early 1800s. I was one of 14 children. There were 7 boys and 7 girls in our family. During that time, give or take one or two children. It did not make much of a difference, because we grew or made everything we had. All that had to take place was we had to plant more, work harder, to create what was needed. Once a child was old enough to do its share of the work the burden for each was the same. We had the second largest family in Merrill Wisconsin the largest family had 21 children. That's just the way it was during that time. More hands were needed to do the work, everything was done by hand. "Manual labor" was the way of the times. Most of the machinery to harvest crops was not invented at that time. During the first three years of my life I remember very little until the age of three. After that everything that happened from then on, is a very vivid picture in my mind. This memory thing started about late 1939 when my older brother's house was being built, by him and my dad. The interesting part of it is the house is sided with slate siding, which must have holes drilled in it, in order to nail it to the boards; you cannot drive nails through stone.

I remember sitting and watching them drill the holes, so they could nail the siding to the sheathing boards, on the outside walls of the house. The slate siding looks good today, like it did and it's 67 years old. The only problem with it is, when a car bounces off of it, it will break. This happened when I was about twenty years old, and was teaching my sister-in-law to drive. She drove all over town without a hitch, and even handled the shoe factory rush that takes place at the shift change, Ivy was her name. You had to know her everything was a giggle if it was serious or otherwise. All went well until she started to enter the driveway at her house. Where on each side there was a hedge that had about three feet of clearance. Ivy brushed the hedge with the car that set off a chain reaction. With first the giggling then she forgot she was driving, and hit the gas, which made the car jump forward. She bounced the car off of the side of the house.

My brother was working nights so he was sleeping on the other side of the wall where the car hit. This is the bedroom location, so when the car hit the wall, and before we passed the window, we saw a set of eyes real wide open with a look of shock peering out of the window. We woke my brother up. Needless to say to this day there are several broken pieces of slate siding on the spot 50 years later, you cannot match the siding. During the building of the house, we kids would get the scraps of wood, and use them as toys. Some of them had shapes that appeared to look like a truck or a car. So we would imagine that's what it was, and make believe that it was just that. We would make the motor sounds when we pushed them around by hand. These were our toys. There was no money to buy toys from the store. The world was in a deep depression, unemployment was 20–30 %. If you had a job the wages were on the order of 12 to 20 cents per hour. We also must point out that you could buy a house with an acre or two of land for $300.00 -$1000.00. The $1000.00 price would buy a large house or an 80-acre farm with house and barns included.

Times were really tough! It is important to understand, we all had a purpose that we had to serve in order to survive. If we wanted something we either created it, or we planted it so it would grow. In other words if we did not grow our food to make it through the winter, we did without. We had to plan very carefully to be able to stretch what we had to survive this meant sometimes we were hungry. We each got our share of what was available, some years many people only had about two thirds of what was needed. The food was budgeted sometimes we went hungry for an entire winter. Can you imagine that concept of not having enough food today with our spoiled society?

If we wanted to go to visit another relative we walked. If Dad was going he hitched up the horse and wagon, then we rode to where we were going. Otherwise we walked even if it was 5 -10 miles. We were very lucky if we had a Bicycle; who could afford one? They were available in one- speed, two peddles, and two wheels, no fancy shifter or any other unnecessary gadgets. So now let's talk about the responsibility assigned to a person, when you were 4–5 years old. When you were able to hold a hoe you were assigned so many hills of potatoes to weed, and nurture so they would yield the maximum number of potatoes, per hill.

For those of you that do not know what a hill of potatoes are, potatoes that are planted in a mound of dirt (a hill) so the soil is loose, yield larger numbers of potatoes per hill. Also because the soil is able to expand easier the potatoes are larger. Therefore you get more food for your effort in less space. Also one of the neighbors that owned a truck would gather up orders for potatoes. From the families in the area, then make the trip to Antigo, Wisconsin, where potatoes were the main crop. The soil in that area was a sandy loam soil that potatoes grew well in. They grew so many potatoes there, that they would have a surplus they could not sell to the market. They would pile the surplus up in large mounds, and spray them with a purple food grade dye. This would designate they were to be used for pig feed there was nothing wrong with the potatoes. The farmers would sell them to whoever came along with the money to pay for them.

The neighbor would buy a truck load of potatoes, and make his deliveries to the people that committed to so many pounds of these surplus potatoes. He sold them for the price he paid for them, plus your share of the fuel cost. The potatoes were priced at about 20 to 25 cents per 100 pounds, depending on how large the surplus was. How did we keep food during the winter? We had no power and no refrigeration; you had to pay attention to each step of this process, if you made a mistake it meant trouble. If the food spoiled, it was too late because the growing season was over. This meant if you did not constantly care for it you did without.

The potatoes were stored in bins in a fruit cellar. A fruit cellar is simply a basement with a dirt floor, this keeps the cellar cool but it does not get cold enough to freeze. This is the ideal condition for keeping fruit. We would have apples, potatoes, carrots, squash and cabbage stored here. The items stored in the fruit cellar had to be inspected for spoilage weekly. We would use the items that were starting to spoil before they had a chance to get too bad.

One must remember one bad apple will spoil the whole batch. This is true! If we got careless, we would have a chain reaction. The food stored in the fruit cellar would spoil. This is all we had and there was no way to replace it. This is how we got our food. This is how it was preserved for the winter use, it is that simple. If we did not take good care of our food we went hungry in the winter. How did we keep our other food during the winter? Three things were key to having enough food for the winter: # 1) Canning/preserving vegetables, wild berries and fruit; # 2)Growing and having a way to keep Potatoes, Cabbage, Pumpkins, Apples, Squash, Nuts and other vegetables. This was done in the fruit cellar. # 3) in the winter in Northern Wisconsin we had natural refrigeration, after Thanksgiving it stayed cold enough until the end of February so meat would keep. So during the winter we butchered Pigs, Beef, canned it or made sausage that would keep in a salt barrel during the summer. Salt barrel sausage does not require refrigeration.

I remember the winters well, we walked about 1 ½ miles to school. There were no snow days, if we would have had snow days, we would not have had school most of the time. During this time we had heavy snows with 1 -2 feet accumulation in one day, with as much as 3–4 feet of snow on the ground. By the way it was shoveled by hand so you could get about. During the spring and summer we would eat the preserved fruit and meat that was prepared last year. The vegetables stored in our fruit cellar, and if we wanted fresh meat we would butcher a chicken or go catch some fish. This is how we survived until the next crop was ready to eat. We had a large garden that was available to eat out of during the summer. This was our snack garden. When we got hungry we would pick some beans, peas or whatever we wanted that was ready to eat at the time. This garden was about ½ acre it, had to be large enough, to provide snacks/lunch for 8 to 10 people at a time. There were 14 children in our family. We all had our chores and there was not a question about if they would be done or not. The neat part of it was there were 2 years between all of us but two that were only a year apart. This meant that there were no more than 8 kids at home at one time.

We younger kids behaved quite well, the older kids kept us in line. We paid attention because if Mom or Dad had to get involved, the lesson lasted a long time: it was pretty severe. There just was too much to do to spend time bickering. You listened, you would speak only when spoken to, did not interrupt at all. You did what you were told to do without question. This worked really well. It is a shame we do not operate that way today. If we did we would have very few problems in our schools. Kids would know where they stood, and what was expected of them. As a result they would feel secure.

We had no lights or running water. We had an outhouse which served as the bathroom summer or winter. All water was pumped from a well by hand. Than carried in buckets to water 5 cows and a horse which were watered in the morning and evening after school. The well also provided water for the chickens, our drinking, cooking and bath water. The hot water was heated in a reservoir on the left side of the kitchen stove or on top of the stove in a copper boiler that held about 10 gallons. This was how it was summer or winter. All cooking and baking was done with a wood-fired cook stove, all heating was with a wood-fired space heater. Now when you stop and think about it, that meant we had to cut, and put up an awful lot of wood, for year-around use. The trees were cut down with a hand operated cross cut saw. The cord wood, the wood was called was cut into usable lengths to fit the stoves. It was cut with a circular saw. The saw was a community piece of equipment that made the rounds with all of the neighbors. Making fire wood was a group effort and hard work. First, the tree was cut down by hand, then the tree was limbed next, the tree was cut in lengths that could be handled. Loaded on a truck or horse-drawn wagon or sleigh, and hauled to an area where it would be cut with the circular saw into cord wood, so it would fit the stoves to heat and cook with.

When a person has a rough way in life, something happens, other than what we want. We have a tendency to whine about it, if we do this self-pity thing, all we need to do is look around. We will see people worse off then we are. So count your blessings! Things are not as bad as you thought. A good example of this is; the dust bowl days in the southwest U.S. during the late 1930's into the early 1940's. Oklahoma, New Mexico, Kansas, Missouri and Arkansas were devastated by a drought. High winds removed as much as 4 inches of their top soil, during the 6–7 years Mother Nature dealt this blow to them. The prairie land was ideal for growing wheat, which was in great demand. A farmer that grew wheat wanted as large a crop, he could get from his land. All of the fence rows were removed, so he had no obstacles in his way, this allowed 100% utilization of the land.

It was not unusual for a field to be 400–600 acres with no wind breaks. Because the wind breaks were removed, when the drought, and high winds came it was natural for the exposed soil to be blown away. How far did the sustained winds carry the soil? I can remember the dust blocking the sun, with so much dust in the air that the sky was colored red. This red dust settled on everything up in Northern Wisconsin 500–700 miles from the affected area for three years. We also had Small pox, Chicken pox, Mumps, Scarlet fever, the Flu, Measles. The nasty disease polio that caused about 1 in 6 children to disappear from our school class causing death in many cases. The least you could hope for if you got Polio was to have severe crippling of your body. I know because I saw it up close and personal. My classmates and brother got it. He was lucky; all that happened to him was a crippled left leg. So just remember that no matter how bad you have it. Just look around and things will not seem as bad as you think. Someone, somewhere, will have it worse than you.

I started school in the fall of 1940. The schools were different than they are now. Classes were larger, but this was easy for the teacher. The children were well disciplined. The teacher was an extension of the parents when it came to a child getting out of line in school. Yes, the teacher could spank your butt or give you a crack on the hand if it were needed. Everyone behaved quite well because there was a consequence for your action. Today in 2006 a child can get by with about anything. Most parents are too busy, too lazy, or too scared of the law our liberal society has imposed on them. The children know that Mom or dad can get in trouble. If they leave a mark on their little butts; the State thinks they know how to raise kids. What a joke!

Just take a look at the lousy job they are doing as the stewards of our resources we trust them with. They steal and squander them away with no consequence for their actions. Go figure! I feel sorry for most of the children today because, they do not know any bounds, nor do most suffer any consequence for their actions. That is why we have the school shootings, the drugs, and most of the other problems we have today. I'm glad I'm passing through this life when I am. I have seen and experienced so many things that make a person appreciate what one has. I am very thankful for all things. If you ever feel sorry for yourself, just look around, and you will find someone much worse off.

Unless you are a fool that will make you really appreciate what you have.

The depression really made the older folks strong as a community. As a nation we all stuck together out of necessity, had we acted individually we would have had many more hardships. Or even worse, we would not have made it, and some did not. We did not have welfare as we know it today. This means we did not have a large part of the population slaves of the state, like those on welfare are. We had honor! We would help each other so we all suffered alike. If a family had a real problem, it would be brought the attention of the pastor of our church, the congregation would all pitch in. This way no one family suffered more than the other.

We did not expect the Government to solve our problems, for starters they could not. It was not the function of the Government, plus they were not capable of doing so. We had Honor, Morality, a hand shake would seal a deal, and your word bound you. We were honest above all else. We did not lock our houses. A thief was a rare creature, plus all locks were skeleton key locks. One key would fit all. Keys were for honest people, crooks would break in if the door was locked or not. I remember this well, in the 1950's after I got out of the Army (I served in Korea). I went home to visit, and all of the doors were locked. Things had changed. There were thieves, breaking into the houses, so people were locking doors.

The only problem was all doors had the skeleton lock, so it was not too effective. Before this time if I was going to visit someone, and they were not home

I would walk in the house, leave a note to tell them, I was here, and would drop back later. I asked what was happening; was told that there were thieves you had to lock your house. You had to get in line, to buy a lock that was different than the skeleton key variety. You had to get on a waiting list, to get a lock to secure your property. What caused this change? Parents wanted to make it better-easier for their children. So they did not discipline them. They were not disciplined, and became more mobile, this combination was devastating to the American way of life. Kids became disobedient at home, this carried over into the school system. A result of this is the legal system started getting involved. Telling parents and teachers spanking a child was bad for their self-esteem. The kids soon found out they could be disruptive in school, and get by with it. This confused the kids, because they were being taught, there really is no right or wrong, no consequence for your actions. It was a matter of what you could get by with, that determined if you were right. Not a good way to do things!

Times were changing. Germany and Japan were in the process of gearing up for war. While talking about peace with different nations, to try to divide and conquer. They were quite successful until December 7th, 1941 when the Japanese invaded Pearl Harbor, destroying many of our ships, and killing about 3000 of our service men, and women. What had happened, is the world was being deceived by the Germans, and at the same time by the Japanese, saying they were peaceful. This betrayal caused the rest of the nations to be lethargic. As a result of this the U.S.A., and the rest of the world were not prepared, for the invasions of many countries by Germany and Japan, which were taking place in Europe and the Far East at the same time.

The main reason this happened is the world was hoping that, what was being said by the deceivers (Germany and Japan) that their actions, would match their words. Both were talking about peace, while gearing up for war, and the rest of the world did nothing to prepare. They wanted to believe all was going to be ok. The U. S did not pay attention until Japan invaded Pearl Harbor. We still wanted to believe that it was not happening. But once the invasion at Pearl Harbor took place we opened our eyes to the truth. Declared war on Japan on December 8th, Germany and Italy on December 11th of 1941; we finally woke up.

This would be the start of the downfall of Japan, Italy and Germany, at a very high cost in lives to all involved. The Jewish people suffered the most. Hitler wanted to eliminate the Jews from the face of the earth. Have a pure perfectly tall blond, blue-eyed German strain of people he believed were superior to all other breeds. Millions of the Jews were killed by Hitler's Germany. Those that escaped the Axis were spread world wide, they did not have a country of their own. Since God sent them the way of the four winds. This action would also end the Great Depression, and would speed up the development process of many of the things we take for granted today. To gear up for war required a major effort on the part of all nations. Need is the brainchild of invention, and the need was great. The needs were beyond all expectations, and were met. History will testify to the results. The enemies were defeated and long since restored. Once America defeated an enemy, we would help them get back on their feet, with hope of making them our ally. The U.S changed all of the industrial power of the nation, to manufacture supplies, to fight the war. Because so many men were off to the battle front, the women had to run most of the home front war effort.

The Second World War started a spiral that still continues. The war to end all wars did not accomplish that. The Rat race continues with no end in sight. I was lucky to be growing up during this time. The experiences I had a witness to these advancements, are something that no generation after my time will be able to have. Maybe they will get to witness things far beyond what has taken place during my time. They will not be able to experience the events I'm about to describe to you.

During the early years of my life hay was cut by hand, or with a horse-drawn wheel driven cycle bar type mower. It was raked by hand or with a dump type rake for those that could afford the equipment. For many of those who could not, the neighbors often shared equipment. Many times the equipment was owned by several neighbors. This was the only way they could afford it. Any heavy work like plowing the fields, cultivating, cutting hay, would be done with the use of horses or with tractors, if available. There was no money to buy tractors during the Great Depression. On the small farms much of the work such as planting, cultivating-hoeing, cutting hay, raking hay, loading hay on the wagon, putting the hay in the barn, digging potatoes was done by hand. All cows were milked by hand until the advent of the milking machine in the late 1940s. I had the privilege of working on a farm when attending Agricultural School. To work with one of the first milk parlors, assembled by a company by the name of De-Laval, De-Laval invented and manufactured milking machines. This farm had 78 milk cows, the year was 1947, and the location was Spring Green, Wisconsin.

Prior to the milk machine, a farm with 20 milk cows was a large farm. Unless the family was large there were not enough hands to do the work. The cows were milked before daylight and after dark so the daylight hours were not wasted. Daylight hours were required to get the other work done, that could not be done when it was dark outside. In my early years many farms did not have electricity (we got electricity about 1942 and had three light bulbs; two in the barn and one in the house). Before that we used Kerosene lanterns as a light source for the chores of milking, cleaning the barn, and others that could be done before daylight. It was very common to work, 12 to 16 hours a day, 6 days a week with time off for Church on Sundays. The cows had to be milked 365 days a year, twice a day, no excuses, if you were sick the chores still had to be done. Generally school homework was done with the use of a Kerosene lantern. Daylight time could not be wasted. Survival was more important than school, if you did not have the necessities of life school was a mute point.

When I was 13 years old my Dad died; he was 56 years old, his death was caused by galvanic poisoning.

He worked in the paper mill and many of the tanks used to make paper were made of galvanized steel. My dad was a welder, and when welding galvanized steel, a poisonous gas is generated. Back in those days it was not realized, that ventilation for one's health was important. It was easier to ignore that fact, because there were no safety laws. The health and welfare of the worker was not considered important, in other words it would cost something to ventilate the area to make it safe. The company could get someone to do the job without the safety considerations in place, because there were no consequences. This sort of thing happened more than we realize. A good example of that is when 3 of the major stock holders-owners of U. S. Steel Company were standing by the hand-fired blast furnaces in the winter.

The men feeding the furnaces were lined up for their turn at feeding, the monster Blast Furnaces in 10 degrees below zero. Dale Carnegie said, "We are losing too many of these poor men to pneumonia because they go from feeding the furnace where it is 120 degrees above to the back of the line where it is 10 below zero." "Why don't we build a warming shack so this does not happen?" One of the 3 owners named Joe K said, "Why should we spend the money to do that?" "We can get more of the Bastards off the street cheaper than building a warming shack? " "Let them die, that is not our problem." This was typical of the times more often than not. Men were begging for jobs with unemployment at 20–25 % or greater.

When my Dad died it created a real hardship at home. So I went to work on a farm for $30.00 a month, plus room and board. $15.00 of that money was given to my mother, to help pay the bills at home. The year was 1948. For this $30.00 a month I worked 6 ¾ days a week, a normal work day was 12 to 16 hours. We had 21 cows to milk by hand for about 6 months. Then the farmer bought a De Laval milking machine. This made life easier only in that the milking machine did that work for us. The rest of the work load stayed the same. I did get 4 hours, two days a week to go to school to study Agriculture. This was a real treat to me it was like a rest period. I worked for this farmer for about 9 months, until he tried to cheat me out of about 1 ½ months pay. This was resolved with the District Attorney getting the Sheriff to take a court order. With several people accompanying us, he threatened to have a Sheriff's sale, with only the chosen people bidding. The farmer paid me and that was the end of that. I then went to work for the neighbor for the same $30.00 a month. This was great because they had no children. I was treated greatly by these folks. I stayed with these folks until my older sister asked me to come live with her and her husband in Ottawa, Illinois.

I would work with her husband, Bob, repairing trucks and trailers. This was real easy, the hours were shorter, the pay much better, and to me the work much easier. After about 6 months Bob's Uncle Terry, asked me if I would work with him, repairing Slot machines. He had a slot machine business, was in need of help. I said yes if it was ok with Bob. I was 15 ¼ years old at this time, was given a 1947 Mercury to drive. Was too young to get a drivers license, it was arranged that I could drive but had to use the car in LaSalle County, Illinois only. If I received a ticket it would be taken care of by local authorities. I only got one parking ticket, before I was old enough to get my drivers license. When I was 16 my driver's license was given to me, by the local authorities on my birthday, without any testing or questioning.

My job with Bob's uncle Terry was to repair the slot machines; this worked out just fine, and was a snap, there was nothing to do, unless the slot machines broke down. The only bad part of the job was, it generally started about 10 a.m. and was on call until the bars closed. This worked out just fine, until Terry wanted to take time off for a month at a time. Terry had to teach me the ropes, because the slot machines had to be emptied at least once a week. The only exception was in some bars, people played the slot machines so much there would be an accumulation of so many coins they would not work. So they had to be emptied once a day, and checked to be sure they were in working order.

From late 1938 to early 1942 we went from most work being done by hand out of necessity, to much of the work being mechanized at a very rapid rate. This was necessary because, there just were not enough hands to support the war effort. Many of the jobs that had been done by men had to be done by women. The men were off fighting the war. Out of necessity the women filled these manufacturing positions, required to make the materials needed to fight the war. Many of the machines that were hand-fed in the past were being automated. One automated machine would, free up a pair of hands or several pairs of hands, for other purposes. Remember, earlier I stated necessity is the brain child of invention. Well we had many necessary, pressing issues that had to be resolved now, to produce the materials to support the war effort. There was no tomorrow in this case. If we had failed, we all would have suffered a fate beyond all you can imagine.

Failure was not an option; success was the only option. Gas, food, and other items needed to feed the troops or meet the needs of the war machine were rationed. We were in an all out war this would change the whole world forever. We were caught napping, our airplanes were bi-wing, slow, obsolete helpless against the Japanese and German planes. We did not see any need to do more prior to the start of the war. Nor could we afford to. Now we had to act quickly to improve our war machinery, in order to meet the need. Once we got the wake up call, we moved forward with such a sense of urgency, that it surprised the enemy. We caught up to them in short order, held our own for several years. After several years we started surpassing the Japanese, and the Germans, in every aspect, our planes were faster, more maneuverable, our subs were greatly improved, and our battleships were becoming superior. We were gaining on the enemy on all fronts, thank God.

For the next several years all of our efforts would be to feed the war monster. We were advancing at such a rapid pace, that if it was not for the war forcing this upon us. We would not have progressed to this point for a generation or two. It is truly amazing what can be accomplished when your back is against the wall.

During the years of 1943–1945 things continued to move forward rapidly. The war was being won on all fronts by the U.S. and our allies. The cost in lives and resources of every kind and description was beyond belief. The same advances were taking place modernizing industry. Medicine was one area that was advancing very rapidly. Because of so many torn bodies the doctors had to experiment with out of desperation in an attempt to save lives. Many new procedures were developed that are used today. The need to act with no restrictions because of the torn bodies requiring attention moved medicine forward by at least 20 years or more in a few years.

The years of 1942 through 1946 saw the U.S. doing things beyond belief on all fronts. This was a need created by the 2nd World War. Not only were our air planes faster, more maneuverable, the ships better, the trucks and cars better. We had developed vastly superior guidance systems for our Planes for take off and landing. They developed better sights for dropping a bomb this improved the percentage of hits on the target. During the struggle to overcome the enemies the U.S. had been working since 1939 on splitting the Atom. The U.S. was doing this, an attempt to develop a weapon 1000 times as powerful as any conventional weapon. It resulted in a bomb that was so devastating that it only took two to bring the Japanese to their senses-knees. This brought the 2nd World War to an end.

The year was 1945 and the first of the two Atomic bombs were dropped on Hiroshima on August 6th at 9:15 A.M; the 2nd bomb was dropped on Nagasaki three days latter on August 9th. Within one minute there was a black cloud of smoke, and debris 1000 feet off the ground, and a white mushroom cloud 20,000 feet high. Needless to say the devastation was beyond belief. Those that were involved that did not die immediately, suffered beyond your wildest imagination. The radiation burns were worse then anything ever seen. The 2nd World War ended on August 15th, 1945 when Japan surrendered. Everyone claimed that it was the War that would end all Wars. Needless to say it turned out to be false.

Since the 2nd World War ended we have had the Korean War, police action as it was called. That was the politically correct way of expressing what was happening. This way no one's feelings were hurt. Since then we have had the Vietnam War, the 1st Gulf War in Iraq, the Afghanistan War and now the 2nd Gulf War in Iraq. Why the U.S. thinks we can change the world by imposing our way of life on them is beyond me. We try to buy their friendship with (foreign aid) international welfare. Because we think our money will buy everything; we just do not learn from our experiences. We are becoming the joke of the world. Our word has become less meaningful because our actions are not what we say.

Our supposed leaders at all levels are two-faced and self-serving and could care less about what happens. Their only care is to get re-elected. They keep increasing the welfare rolls (making those on welfare that do not deserve it slaves of the state). In other words they are using our tax dollars to buy votes. National and international welfare will be the ruination of our way of life, along with our liberal self-serving wasteful ways, and our lack of morals.

A large percentage of the U.S. population is turning into a God-less, fat, lazy bunch. It is disgusting! If we do not change our ways soon, we will have a painful day of reckoning. We over spend, and over indulge ourselves. We have a Government that thinks there is no end to what they can spend. All they have to do is turn up the speed of the printing presses to make more money. At a point in time the inflated money will be worthless. If the supposed leaders want to find out how well that way of life works. All they need to do is let me handle their household budget for a year. At the end of the year I would return it to them in the same shape that our federal budget is in. I do not believe they would like that but. I believe that is the only way the fools will get the message. What do you think?

We have experienced many changes from about 1938 to 1945 and will now try to organize the progression of the developments for you, there are many. We will start with a brief of some of the developments before my time so things can be put in a proper prospective. Automobiles were available to those who could afford them in numerous brands during the 1920s. These times were known as the roaring 20s. The 20s were called that because things were going well. Everyone was making money, and spending it like there was no tomorrow. Let the good times roll! You will see the advancements that were made out of necessity during the 2nd World War, and the same thing took place during the 1st World War. There were Airplanes, Submarines, Trucks, Tanks, Ships and many of these things available to fight the 1st World War. They were just much cruder versions. They were the first or the forerunners of things to come. The U. S. entered the 1st, World War, the war to end all Wars in 1917. It ended in 1918, although the war had been going on for four years in Europe.

The 1st World War brought on the start of the industrial revolution, and the good times known as the roaring 20s. This lasted until the stock market crash of October 24th, 1929 (black Thursday). It was called the roaring 20s because everyone was living the way we do now, way beyond their means. This type of spending can only last so long, there is only so much air that a balloon will hold, then it bursts, just as we can only have so much inflation. Then the good life ends because, we pumped too much paper-money into the market. A result the dollar loses its value. Just like the over-inflated balloon that burst, the over inflated dollar caused our bubble to burst, so to speak. Let the good times roll! In other words you cannot spend more then you make forever, it just will not work. The people of the U.S. are trying. The longer it continues the worse it will be when all hell breaks loose. The Great Depression touched everyone's life. Those that stayed in the market lost everything. Those that cashed out were in good shape. Cash was king and very few people had it. We will call the next stock market crash the Greater Depression. It will be much worse.

We had cars with such names as Whippet, Hudson, Studebaker, Nash, Dodge, Chrysler, Willy's, Elk, Plymouth, Ford, Chevrolet, Franklin, Opal and several more I cannot think of. America was the land of the automobile. Ford put the first assembly line together, and passed the 1,000,000 mark in production of the Model T, also known as the Tin Lizzy. In 1928 the first T.V. sets were available at a cost of $75.00; prohibition was in full swing. Prohibition was found to be a big mess. It could not be enforced so there was talk of getting rid of it. The year is 1929. The first airplane flights of any real distance or duration were taking place. A military airplane was in the air for 150 hours. This was accomplished with in- flight refueling, and opened up flights from the East coast of the U.S. to France.

The year is 1929 and the Arabs and Jews are fighting. The Arabs and Jews have been in conflict for about 2000 years. So what's new here? I think we have heard this one before. Ever since God spread the Jews to the four winds, they have been without a home. No country wants to accept them as their own. It is *Biblical* that they return to their homeland of Israel. The U.N. is formed on June 26th, 1945 the first official session is opened on June 10th. In 1948 the U.N. declared Israel a state. The same time the Arabs swore to remove them from the face of the earth. You know they have been trying to do so ever since.

Black Thursday, October 24th, 1929 the stock market crashed losing 25% of its value in several hours. Stockholders were telling their brokers to sell at whatever price they could get for their stock. You could hardly give them away because the shares were losing value quickly. Some stock holders committed suicide. They had speculated with everything they had and lost it all. Many people lost everything accept the shirt on their back. I found out when I was about 12 years old that my Dad lost everything in the crash. My Granddad on my Mother's side was wealthy. He bailed my dad out so we had a place to live. Times were tough for all. They would get worse things were just starting to unravel.

This was the start of the Great Depression that would last until the 2nd World War came along and bailed things out. If most people had lived in the city it would have been worse. They would not have had a place to grow their food. We grew our food and the transition from being comfortable. To being slightly less comfortable was not too great a shock because we had a way out. There are three strikes against the people of today: #1). They do not have a place to grow their food; #2). Most of them would not know how to do the job if they had the land. Someone else has always grown what they eat; all they had to do is go to the store and buy it. Except now they would have no money to do so. # 3) Most of the people of today are too lazy to do what they need to do to survive. Watching T.V. and playing computer games is not a skill that will be useful for survival. I hate to say it but we are raising a bunch of brats because the parents will not get off their butts. Do what needs to be done. Or the government has them too scared to do the job because of the laws passed regarding disciplining a child.

I have numerous black friends; they are super they will do whatever they can to help you. Just as I have done for them. They do not see color anymore than I do. Why not? Because they are good moral, ethical, down- to-earth, Christian people. This is how they were raised. If we take a look at why there is a problem with Black and White all we need to do is look at the prison population. It will tell the story straight up. We have about 60% of us supporting the other 40%. The Black people are about 17% of the population in America. Two factors come into play here. One the prison population is mostly Black. Two more black people are on welfare then White people. Now you can see the depth of the problem, this is just plain wrong. What is the root cause? Mostly laziness it is that simple. You have Black, White and Mexican men running around making kids they do not support. Why not? Because they have not been taught a better way, it is easy to get welfare, and the women increase their income by having more babies. Our tax dollars are being used to support them. Our elected officials are making them slaves of the state (buying their vote) with our tax money. Can you imagine these people not having things handed to them?

Moving on, the year is 1930. Prohibition is 10 years old. Alcoholism is rampant in the nation; On January 15th -1920 a law was passed prohibiting the sale of Alcoholic beverages. The reason the law was passed is people were dying from Alcohol poisoning. Ten years later the problem is six times as bad. The death rate from alcoholism is six times greater then it was before prohibition was law. There is a bill on the house floor to revoke the law. It made things worse. It is (noted) free people cannot be prohibited from doing some things. There is a lesson to be learned here. At this time in America there is much talk about banning smoking. It will not work. All a complete ban (prohibition) would do is open a Black Market for Tobacco. We have to learn from our past experiences. Don't we?

Major world powers are looking to reduce war preparedness. This is an attempt to lessen the threat of war. Stalin has collectivized the farmers. Now the Russians all work for the good of and for the state. Another lesson in Communism, under the system all property and livestock become property of the state. New York installs traffic lights to protect pedestrians. Five great powers sign a naval treaty to limit the arms they may have. They feel this is a way to reduce the threat of more wars. Babe Ruth the baseball player makes more money per year, than president Hoover does. The Nazi's party is the 2nd largest political party in Germany; this is the start of the rise to power of Hitler. Hoover seeks aid to combat the depression. The depression deepens. 1930 is not a good year for the world.

1931 jobless in the U. S. reaches over 4,000,000 with 360,000 more unemployed in one month. In Europe it is worse, with a higher percent of the population unemployed. May 1st the Empire State Building will open it is the tallest building in the world. International welfare is started when Hoover proposes to allow the Germans to delay, paying for the damage they caused in the 1st World War. Banks are failing world wide, particularly overseas. London's unemployed are rioting. They are insisting that the English government put them on the dole (welfare). Some of the rioters are believed to be commies. A

U.S. Submarine attempts to reach the North Pole. Civil war threatens in Kentucky hungry families roam the area begging for food. Those that are working in the coal mines make $9 to $12 per week are deeply in debt to the company stores. This fact was the fore runner of the song "St Peter, don't call me I can't go, I owe my soul to the company store." Things are really tough and a big mess at the end of 1931.

1932 starts out in bad shape. Japan has taken over Shanghai and Manchuria. The U.S. threatens to get involved Italy and England have sent troops. Hoover asks for and receives $2,000,000,000 to try to shore up industry. Things are much worse than they were. Hitler is gaining popularity. He is talking long and loud about "a chicken in every pot and A Volkswagen in every driveway"; the people are desperate so they believe him. The Atom is split by two British scientists. Hitler's Nazis double the number of seats in legislative elections in Germany. The number of unemployed jumps to 11,000,000 in the U.S. the depression deepens. Jimmy Walker resigns as the Mayor of New York City. He was caught with his hands in the cookie jar, so to speak. The supposed leaders were crooks even back then, but not in the numbers we have today. The Yankees win the World Series in four straight games. Franklin D. Roosevelt wins a land slide victory for president of the U.S. on, Nov. 8th with an electoral vote of 472 to Hoover's 59. We get a new look at how to solve the Great Depression, Roosevelt says get a plan, implement it, see if it works, and if it does not change it quickly, if it is not working. He stated he was waging a war against the four Horsemen of the present Republican party of Destruction, Delay, Deceit and Despair. He calls for many public works programs to put people to work.

1933, the situation has not improved. Our Allies are plagued with staggering debts. This crisis has been triggered by the world-wide depression which has worsened. Hitler is named German Chancellor. All of his opponents fear him, but feel he will be less dangerous if he is in office. There are bloody riots in the streets almost daily, it seems Germany is on the brink of a civil war. Most Germans feel Hitler will purge the country of the communists quickly as he can; some have already been shot to death. Socialism-communism is threatening many countries. The people are desperate and the situation is getting worse. Feb. 15th there was an attempt on President Roosevelt's life. Four people with him are wounded, but he escapes untouched.

Japan walks out on the League of Nations, following a discussion about the occupation of China. March 10th an earthquake kills 123 people in the L. A. California area, and injures 4150. March 20th Hitler's Nazis have arrested so many political opponents that, Germany opens the first concentration camps. That month alone 15,000 were arrested. March 4th Roosevelt makes his famous statement "the only thing we have to fear is fear itself." This seemed to breathe new hope into the people. Dictatorial power is granted to Hitler and gives him the power to make laws to suit himself. No one dare question him unless they wanted to be shot or worse.

Roosevelt takes the U.S. money off of the Gold

standard because the dollar is fluctuating in value so wildly. The economists feel it is not dignified to have Gold backing our dollar any longer. The private ownership of Gold is outlawed. The Gold content value of the dollar is now 50 % of what it was. In essence this doubles the number of dollars available immediately with the stroke of the pen. The first welfare bill is passed in the form of farm aid. The Nazis make bonfires of all books that disagree with their thinking. Hitler breaks up all trade unions, and the labor leaders are arrested. The Nazis are the only political party in Germany. June 16th the U.S. passes a bill called the NRA (National Recovery Administration) this is a make work program to build roads in the U.S. and to start building ships. Both were needed and it would put people to work. June 23rd big government spending makes millions of jobs. Unemployment went from 13.4 million to 12.7 million in April. Aviation is declared safe and practical the, all metal Boeing 247 aircraft first flew in Feb. It would carry 10 passengers. The Nazis pass a law to purify the German race, and only Blue-Eyed-Blond haired Aryan people are allowed to breed. This is Hitler's attempt to fulfill his fantasy of a superior race of people. The Nazis are sending many Jews to prison camps.

Sept. 30th in America 3.5 million families are on the relief rolls, the bread and soup lines are long, there are many needy. Labor unions are gaining strength, and employers are taking advantage of the situation. They are not providing safety measures for workers. Dec. 5th prohibition ended, it was a program that did not work; and public drinking of alcoholic beverages is now legal. Jan. 30th the jobless join the Civilian Conservation Corps which is known as the CCC. The CCC workers are to rebuild the Nation's great outdoors. They are paid $30.00 a month plus room and board. Roosevelt devalues the dollar to 60 cents, setting the price of Gold at $35.00 per ounce. This move created about 2.8 billion new dollars 2 billion of these dollars will be used to bolster the dollar on the international markets. Communism is on the move in, some cases it is called the Social Democratic party to make it acceptable. The redistribution of money or social welfare is viewed as a way out of the depression.

1934 Hitler is doing make-work projects in Germany in an attempt to reduce unemployment. Hitler is also consolidating his power base. Some of his leaders attempted a revolt they were given the opportunity to commit suicide, if they did not they were executed on the spot. Hitler has stopped paying all foreign debts. The U.S. is stuck with carrying the load. Out of a half billion dollars owed by 15 countries only Finland is paying back the money owed. In several parts of the U.S. workers are striking, and dozens of workers are killed as the strikes turn violent. Colonel Roscoe Turner flies from L.A. to N.Y. in 10 hours setting a new speed record. Nov. 6th the Democrats scored big at the polls, because the public supported Roosevelt's New Deal. Taking money from (the thrifty) and giving it to the other folks, welfare. Stalin is on the move in the U.S.S.R. Killing his rivals as he gains power. Communism, Mao Tse-tung is on the move in China, and the Great Depression is still with us.

1935 Sept.6ᵗʰ of this year I was born in Merrill, Wisconsin, I was number 12 of what would be a family of 7 boys and 7 girls. Storm clouds are gathering over Europe as Hitler starts military conscription. This move is a breach of the treaties signed by Germany to ease tensions. Hitler gears up the German military and Mussolini follows his lead because the two are in cahoots with each other. The U.S. is hit by a dust storm that covers western Kansas, eastern Colorado and western Oklahoma. Nearly all of Texas and parts of New Mexico were having breathing problems. Many cattle are dying and there are many cases of dust pneumonia among children. The dust storm covers half of the U.S. with most crops wiped out. I remember the "Dust Bowl days" the dust blocked the sun it, was hazy in Wisconsin for about 3 years. The distance Merrill, Wisconsin is from the dust storm is 6–7 hundred miles red dust covers the surface of everything in our area. The Dust Bowl days lasted for about 4 years before the rains came.

The Great Depression is in full bloom! The National Industrial Recovery Act which. Allowed the government to set wages and hours of work is replaced, with the Works Progress Association or WPA as it was known. This was a new weapon used to provide jobs for needy Americans, and that was most of the people in the U.S. during this time. The Japanese are on the move in China. July 5ᵗʰ a new law is passed in the U.S. that supports the rights of workers to join unions. The Nazi repression of Jews is intensified, and gangs of Nazi bullies are chasing Jews. They are calling out for the Destruction of all Jews. The U.S. warns the

Soviets to stay out of America because the communists are trying to interfere in U.S. internal affairs. August 4th President Roosevelt signed into law the Social Security Act, keeping his 1932 campaign promise. September 3rd Sir Malcolm Campbell, the British speed ace exceeds 300 miles per hour, in a special car. Howard Hughes flies an airplane at 350 miles per hour for a new speed record. A new airplane, the DC3 carries 21 passengers, flies at 160 miles per hour; the original version had 14 beds in it to compete with the railroads. The Movies offer an escape from hard times. The movies of this era are movies that did not need to be rated, they were good, clean family type movies, Hollywood used to be a moral and ethical place.

1936 Adolf Hitler opens the winter Olympics. The Volkswagen, "the people's car," makes its debut. The Germans admire the Ford assembly line method of manufacturing cars. The Nazis enter Rhineland and Ethiopia, and the Italian forces defeat the Ethiopian forces. The Tel Aviv-Jaffa district of Palestine has been wracked with violence. The Arabs are resisting the entry of the Jewish people being displaced by the Germans. Jesse Owens, an American athlete, is the star performer at the Olympics in Berlin. Hitler insists the Negro race is inferior. Jesse Owens was a Black American, and he defeated German Athletes much to the dismay of Hitler. Hitler left the Stadium to save face because he felt the pure German Aryan people were superior people. Jesse Owens was a great one! Roosevelt is elected President for the 2nd time. The Burlington railroad's Zephyr train set a new Long distance speed record. It traveled from Chicago to Denver at an average speed of 83.3 miles per hour.

1937, Jan. 20th President Roosevelt was sworn in as President. He heralds the nation's steady climb out of the depression, and states I still see one third of the nation's people are underprivileged. Feb. 6th Du-Pont patents a new thread called nylon. April 27th German warplanes bomb Spain. Hitler wants to teach the Spanish a lesson to, either join us or that would be their fate. Hundreds of people are killed. Joseph Stalin purges the Russian military of opposition, and he has 8 Soviet Generals shot. Jan. 30th the Japanese are on the move in China. They launched a major attack with tanks and bombers on several fronts.

Aug. 22nd the Japanese bombers shatter Shanghai in heavy fighting, and are poised to take over the city. Japan is labeling some of the goods they sell to other countries made in the USA. So they can sell them, their products are cheap and shoddy. Oct. 30th the British are restricting the Jews from entering Palestine, and impose quotas. Sept. 5 the Nazis are holding rallies they, claim the Jews are murdering people that are not Jews. Nov. 29th the Nazis are removing children from households because many parents are refusing to teach their children Nazis ideology. If they do not teach them Nazis ideology, Hitler feels they will turn out to be enemies of the state. Mexico is nationalizing all oil lands, and they seize all lands leased to American and British oil companies. December 22nd the Japanese sink U.S. ships, and claim they mistook them for Chinese. Then render immediate medical treatment to the five Americans that were wounded.

The year is 1938 and the world is in turmoil. The Germans and Japanese are gearing up for war while they talk peace. Even though the signs are there most nations want to believe that everything will be ok. So they sit on their laurels, doing nothing to prepare. The U.S. still has 8,000,000 jobless, and the number could well be over 10,000,000. 1 in 5 Americans are still unemployed. It was noted that the situation, has worsened since these figures came out; the Great Depression is still in full swing. Feb. 4th Hitler promotes himself to military chief this gives him unprecedented power. Now he has complete control of every aspect of everything of every nature, national or international. March 15th the Soviets are executing any people that disagree with the Socialist ideology. Mexico seizes 17 American and British oil companies. Their 6 year plan calls for the mechanization of industry, and to this day in 2006 the Mexicans still have not improved their lot. There is too much graft-dishonesty in the country. March 14th Adolf Hitler is hailed as the Nazis take Austria. The German leader who left Austria in his youth a penniless artist was cheered by thousands. He returned to Vienna to pronounce the Anschluss or union of the country with Germany. May 29th, in the U.S. there are many union strikes of various large companies. There is a major labor movement going on, people want what they feel is their fair share of the wealth. Many of the strikes turn violent. The strike at the Goodyear rubber plant left 100 injured today.

Joe Louis, the heavy weight champion boxer of the world is going strong. He floors Max Schmelling, the

German boxer in the first round. I listened to most of his fights, he was great! That is I listened to his fights when the old Motorola radio that we had would allow me to. The reception left much to be desired. The speaker was about 18 inches in diameter you had to put your head inside it to be able to hear the fight. The sound was but a mere whisper, at best. June 15th the minimum wage is set at 40 cents per hour with the maximum work week set at 44 hours. About 1/3 of the people that do have jobs are employed in government make-work projects. The Great Depression is still at full strength with unemployment still at 20% or greater. September 30th there was a four power conference in Munich Germany with the British, French, Italians and Germans where they reached a peace agreement. The British Prime Minister stated. "I believe this will bring peace in our time." Just a week prior to this conference the British Prime Minister appeased Hitler by giving in to Hitler's demands. Germany warned the British that the Germans had more war planes than they do. Hitler's Germany is on the move, and takes over Sudetenland which is in Czechoslovakia. Oct. 9th the Yanks beat the Cubs for the third World Series baseball championship in a row. Nov. 7th the Jews are accused of financing the 1917 Russian revolution. The Germans are using all means at their disposal, to justify what they are doing, and planning to do to the Jews. In America a new hero, Superman, is created by Jerry Siegel and Joe Schuster.

1939 is the year where I start to remember everything. I'm 3 going on four years old. My first vivid memory is of the siding of my brother's house. The siding had to have holes drilled in it to fasten it to the wall. It was Italian slate. "You cannot drive a nail in rock," I was told when I asked what they were doing. Jan. 28th the Germans split the Atom releasing 200M volts of energy. This was announced at a meeting of theoretical physicists in Washington by Enrico Fermi of the University of Rome. Enrico said the enormous amount of energy was released in an experiment by Otto Hahn, a German physicist. James J. Hines the district leader in New York City took bribes to cover up for Dutch Schultz, a racketeer. He was indicted, convicted and sent to prison.

Feb. 22nd the American Nazis party holds a rally in New York. (The German-American Bund) staged what they called an "Americanism" rally. Denouncing the nation's Jews, for their hatred of German Nazis and National Socialism. March 15th eight hours after the German troops entered the Capital of what used to be the Czechoslovak republic. The swastika was raised over the castle of the Bohemian kings. Germany dominates yet another country in a matter of hours, and the rest of the world watches in silence. Mussolini's Italian troops invade Albania the official theme is progress and peace. With what has been happening everyone knew that Europe was on the brink of war. In April, Britain and Poland sign The "Mutual Aid Treaty." May 22nd Italy and Germany sign "Pact of Steel" which binds them for 10 years economically, politically and militarily with the declared objective of reorganizing Europe. Promoting the two powerful nations and creating a "just peace" in the world." They agreed that Germany would rule on land, Italy would rule on the sea in times of war. This agreement alarmed the rest of Europe. An American sub sinks; 33 saved, 26 lost. The cause of the sinking was a, valve was left open when the sub made a dive causing it to fill with water. Some 900 Jewish refugees from Germany were stranded on a ship when going from port to port trying to find a home for them, and they are refused entry by nation after nation. War is threatened over Danzig Hitler, wants to absorb Danzig into the Reich. Britain and France warn Hitler if he does, this it may precipitate another war; Hitler shows no concern over the warning. His military leaders have already assembled a strike force in preparation for an invasion. Standard Oil Co. is to drill for oil in Saudi Arabia the, Saudis have granted a concession for standard oil to drill the entire kingdom. August 3rd, hope for peace has evaporated throughout Europe when the conflict deepens. Germany attacks Poland, Great Britain has begun to mobilize her fleet, and is operating with emergency powers granted by their house of Parliament.

Thousands of school children have been evacuated from London to the safety of the countryside. The French children have also been whisked out of Paris to safety. August 10th, the U.S. has placed the largest peacetime order for airplanes and it appears that war is imminent. F.D.R. changes the date for Thanksgiving, the holiday would leave a larger gap between it and Christmas. September 30th the Nazis invade Poland even though, France and Britain warned them they would get involved in the fight, if they invaded Poland. The Nazis split Poland with Russia. Sept 30th Britain and France declare war on Germany. This follows the quick German invasion, and takeover of Poland.

The U.S denounced the aggression, but declared they would stay neutral. Most other nations still do not believe there will be a war that will involve them. Oct. 20th Hitler makes peace pleas England, and France reject the peace pleas. Hitler is bristling. The Germans say they have rejected the "Fuhrer's hand of peace." France stated that "there will be no lasting peace until Hitler is defeated." A pact is signed between Britain, France and Turkey which makes Hitler furious. Hitler warns Turkey they are playing with fire. Oct.14th, the Germans sink two English ships with more than 800 dead as a result; the ships are the Royal Oak, and the British Liner Athenia. The British thought the Royal Oak was, impervious to torpedoes because it was fitted with extra heavy armor.

Oct. 30th, the British report the Nazis are being cruel to all prisoners Jew and non-Jew alike. The prisoners are being tortured beyond imagination. Many prisoners are bound to a tree with their feet barely touching the ground, then kicked, and hit with large sticks and clubs. Most die a horrible death, a result of this treatment. Nov 30th, the Soviets attack Finland, the war deepens. Nov. 8th six people were killed, and Hitler escapes with his life when a plot to kill him failed. Dec.15th the movie *Gone with the Wind* opens. Dec.30th the German ship Graf Spee was severely damaged but limped back to port. On orders from Hitler it was blown up. The commander Langsdorff wrote a note to the Nazis Admiralty and committed suicide.

The year is 1940. The Russians, the Italians, and the

Germans are invading country after country without reason. More and more countries are drawn into the war. Jan 19th the Russians have invaded Finland, after 6 weeks of fighting they seem desperate to end the conflict. The Fins baffle them with their fierce fighting. The Swedes, Norwegians and the Danish are helping the Finish they, say the Russians will not be allowed to attack the Fins from their countries. The Russians are so frustrated, it is said they are fighting each other. Many of them were trapped in the snow, and are captured. They are exhausted, and suffering from severe frostbite. Feb. 26th, the British seize a German tanker in Norway six Germans were killed in the assault. Feb. 27th the Soviets launch a new attack on the Finns, and take a fierce pounding. The Finns appeal to the rest of the world for help as they make their last stand. March 16th the American Undersecretary of State came to Europe to talk peace, what he found was that a wider war was inevitable. He has been trying to get all countries involved to sit down, and talk peace. He warned Hitler that the U.S. would react, if he continued his military advances. Hitler lectured him that he had a need to protect the German borders. The British and French are not interested in talking peace. But the Italians were they were not prepared for this war. Benito Mussolini encourages the American Secretary, to do what he can to prevent the war from dragging on.

March 13th the Finns surrender to Russia after 3 ½ months of a brutal fight. March 18th Mussolini meets with Hitler. The Germans, the Russians and the Italians lay plans for the formation of a three way understanding of power. The understanding would aim at a new order of Europe. April 9th the Nazis entered Scandinavia, and so surprised were the Danes, they offered no resistance. April 1st an anti-war coalition is formed in the U.S. some Americans oppose getting involved in the European war, as they are calling it. The FCC is developing Television rules, commercial T.V. is about to take off. May 10th, Churchill is now Prime Minister of Britain, he states he has nothing to offer "but blood, toil, tears and sweat." He was a constant critic of Britain's policy of appeasement of Hitler.

May 10th, hundreds of German planes attack Belgian and Dutch cities. The Nazis expand their rein of terror across Europe, taking over country after country. May 24th, Roosevelt promises to train 50,000 airplane pilots for war and America prepares for direct involvement in the conflict. May 28th, Holland and Belgium surrender to the Nazis, the news comes two weeks after the Netherlands surrendered to the Nazis; France opposed the surrender. The Dutch commander in chief asked his troops to give up, to "prevent more bloodshed and annihilation." All of Europe is intimidated by the Nazi's actions. June 4th, the Allied forces escape annihilation at Dunkirk, after the ruthless, and successful German advance. For some unexplained reason Hitler orders a halt to the attack; this allows the British Royal Navy to evacuate the 340,000 allied troops, thus avoiding imminent annihilation. June 14th, German troops parade through Paris France, French men, and women wept openly. The Germans are battering the French troops on all fronts. June

17th, Soviet Russia occupies three Baltic, States Russia takes advantage of the world's preoccupation with Germany's conquests in Western Europe. It is stated Hitler may have approved the actions during treaty negotiations last year.

FDR accuses Italy of a stab in the back by, allying the country with Germany against France, and Great Britain. He states the U.S. will give its support-aid to France, and Great Britain. June 18th, the French general Charles De Gaulle urges the French not to surrender. June 22nd, the French sign an armistice with the Nazis. Hitler has the signing of the armistice take place, in the same rail car where he felt Germany was humiliated, after its 1st World War defeat in 1918. July 29th, the British are bombed by the Germans, the British down 17 German fighter planes and only lost 1. The British are turning the tide of the war giving the Germans some of their own medicine. The RAF hits 100 German cities. August 20th, Rader guards Britain, the Rader can detect enemy aircraft at a distance of 75 miles. This allows time to get planes in the air to meet the attackers.

August 26th, the RAF hits Berlin, astonishing the Germans, the British retaliate for a raid the Germans made on London. Sept. 30th, the Germans are making an all-out effort with the incessant heavy bombing of London. The Germans lose two fighter planes for every one of the RAF planes British planes - pilots were superior. Sept. 27th, the Japanese join the Axis pact. The Japanese link with Germany and Italia signing a tripartite military alliance. The Germans and Italians move toward the "new order of Europe" plan and Japan's right to establish "a new order in Eastern Asia." This will affect the course of the European war and the world in general. October 29th the first draft number is drawn in the U.S. this is the start of military conscription. Oct. 30th, unable to invade Britain, Hitler makes changes in his war policy. He wants France and Spain to fight with him, and holds separate meetings with them in an attempt to move them in this direction. The Spanish go for the deal, France refuses to help Hitler.

Oct. 10th, the Germans bomb St. Paul's church. Proving nothing is sacred to them. Oct. 28th Italy invades Greece, the war spreads. Nov 29th the Nazis hit British cities, and Hitler meets with the Russians in, an attempt to get them to join the Axis. This would be a great setback for the British if it happened. Nov 5th, Roosevelt is in for his third term as President of the U.S. Nov.11th, the Jeep makes its debut as a General purpose military vehicle. Dec. 29th, FDR calls America the "arsenal of democracy" he is determined to keep the U.S. out of the war. The thinking is we will supply the other countries with war materials, let them do the fighting. So we are supplying Britain, and France with war material on, what is called the lend-lease program, with the cost to be repaid at a latter time.

The year is 1941. Feb. 4th Bulgaria accepts Nazi's occupation, and Yugoslavia rejects the Nazi deal. The Yugoslavia government arrests those that signed a new treaty with the Axis. April 10, the U.S. takes control of Greenland, because the Germans have been making reconnaissance flights in, the North Atlantic. Greenland is a Danish colony, and Denmark has been captured by the Nazis. April 17th The Nazis invade Yugoslavia smashing Belgrade because Hitler wants revenge for the earlier rejection of the treaty the Germans offered to them. April 27, The Greek army capitulates to the Germans, the Germans moved swiftly, and sweep into Athens. April 8th, the Supreme Court rules Negroes are entitled to travel first class on trains. May 27th, the British got some revenge for the sinking of the British warship, The Hood. They caught up to, and sunk the German warship, the Bismarck. May 10th, Germany is again trying to divide the world into two spheres of influence. Hitler's right hand man tries to convince Britain that's the way it must be.

May 27th, things are getting closer to home President, Roosevelt declares an emergency, an attempt to avoid declaring war. May 23rd, the greatest heavyweight boxer ever, Joe Louis wins his 17th title defense. What a great one he was!

Things are swinging back and forth with the, British are starting to win some of the battles with the Germans and Italians. June 16th, a Japanese oil tanker is prevented from returning to, Japan with its cargo of 252,000 gallons of oil. June 30th, there was a massive Nazi attack on Russia. Hitler attempts to fulfill his dream of Lebensraum, or living space for the German people. He said the reason for attacking Russia is, Russian-British cooperation threatening the safety of Europe. July 16th, the Germans are battering the Russian troops, meet little resistance on, the march toward Leningrad. Hitler is already planning how to reorganize Russia. June 7th, the U.S. takes charge of Iceland this, is a move to prevent German occupation of the island. August 26th, the British and Russians invade Iran the, purpose is to remove German influence. Sept. 6th, the Jews must wear the Star of David to mark them Jew. They must have a black sign sewn below the Star of David (Jew) and it must always be visible. Sept. 4th an unidentified Sub fires on a U.S. ship. Sept, 4, Nazis encircle Leningrad Hitler, plans to starve the city to death. Oct. 20, Residents of Moscow are in a state of panic as the Germans approach. Adolf Hitler says the Russians are surrounded, the war is almost over. Oct. 30th, the German subs hit two American ships, and one is sunk. November 13[th,] a British carrier is sunk by an Italian torpedo.

Nov. 29th, the Japanese, and U.S. are holding talks, tensions increase between the two nations. Tojo says the British, and Americans are exploiting the Asian people, and must be purged with vengeance. December 5th, snow, cold, and the Soviet determination stopped the German Blitzkreig (attack) dead in its tracks. Dec. 6th, Britain declares war on Finland, Rumania, and Hungary when they ignored an ultimatum to, stop their hostilities toward Russia. We must remember that Russia was, fighting the Germans alongside the British at this time. Dec. 25, British Hong Cong surrenders to the Japanese forces, they are overpowered. One must remember that America is not involved in the war because at this time, we still want to believe, there will be peace. The British are spread really thin by, the Germans, and Japanese attacks on their friends around the world.

December 7th, the Japanese attack Pearl Harbor with, some 360 Japanese warplanes, pulverizing the

American military base. Thousands are killed. Many more wounded. Now America declares war on Japan on December 8th, and on December 11th war is declared on the Axis partners, Germany and Italy. Roosevelt declares we assure victory, over the forces of evil in the world, or there will be no justice. Our forces at Pearl Harbor were, enjoying the good life, and were caught off guard. They were playing golf or generally goofing off, when the Japanese hit the base at Pearl Harbor. They were warned that the attack would take place; they just did not know when, and were not alert. Now America is plunged into war around the world, because we were complacent, are not too well prepared. Roosevelt asks for the biggest budget ever, to fight the war, and taxes must, be raised to finance it.

Feb. 15th the British surrender Singapore to the Japanese. The advantage belongs to the Japanese they have more, and superior airplanes, ships, and were preparing for war, while the rest of the world did not believe it would get this bad. Also we must remember 9–11. It happened because we were complacent. We must be prepared, we must be diligent or we will pay the price because, the countries of the world are, able to reach us within hours. We will not escape as we did during the 2nd World War the, oceans-distance is no advantage. Do not forget we are vulnerable! Support strengthening our military, and our resolve to overcome the evil that pervades some people of this world. Support our president, and our troops above all else during this time of conflict. We are all Americans and must be united as one "United we stand, divided we fall."

Just to make sure you know what brought America to the brink. Also what caused us to wake up, pull our head out of the sand, and caused America to pay attention. To what Germany and Japan were doing while we were making believe, if we ignored things, everything would be ok. Well on December 7th, 1941 we got a wake up call. The Japanese launched a surprise attack against the U.S. forces that we had stationed at Pearl Harbor, Hawaii. By planning the attack on a Sunday the Japanese commander, Admiral Nagumo hoped that he would catch the entire fleet in port. As luck would have it, the Aircraft Carriers, and one of the Battleships were not in port. The USS Enterprise was returning from Wake Island. It had just delivered some aircraft. The USS Lexington was ferrying aircraft to Midway. In spite of his latest intelligence reports his most important targets were not in port. The Commander continued the attack with a force of six aircraft carriers and 423 aircraft. He launched the first wave of attack at 0600 hours using 183 fighters and torpedo bombers, striking the fleet at Pearl Harbor, the airfields in Hickam, Kaneohe and Ewa, Hawaii.

The second strike was launched at 0715 hours, and hit the same targets. When it was over, the U.S. losses were: US Army killed 218, wounded 364; US Navy 2,008 killed, wounded 710; US Marines 109 killed, 69 wounded; Civilians 68 killed, wounded 35 for a total 2,403 killed, and a total of 1,178 wounded. Here is a list of the Battleships that were damaged or sunk: The USS Arizona, USS Oklahoma, USS California, and the USS West Virginia were sunk. The USS Nevada was beached to prevent it from sinking and was later repaired. The USS Pennsylvania, the USS Maryland and the USS Tennessee all sustained light damage. Here is a list of the Cruisers that were damaged or sunk: the USS New Orleans, USS San Francisco and the USS Detroit. USS Helena and the USS Honolulu all sustained light damage. The USS Raleigh was heavily damaged but later repaired. Here is a list of the Destroyers that were damaged or sunk: USS Helm (light damage), USS Downs and the USS Cassin were destroyed and the USS Shaw had very heavy damage. Here is a list of ships that were damaged but later repaired, the USS Ogala, a mine layer, USS Curtiss, a seaplane tender, USS Vestal, a repair ship, and the USS Sotoyomo, a harbor tug. Also 188 aircraft were destroyed. The American forces were playing golf and generally having a good time before the Japanese attack.

We did not want to believe that something like this would happen. We had our head buried in the sand we, wanted to believe that everything would be ok If we did not get involved. This happened even though we had intelligence that it was going to happen we, just did not know when so we were caught napping. What a price to pay for being a pacifist. Let's not forget Pearl Harbor, any more than we can afford to forget 9/11. If we do forget we will pay a much higher price the next time. We know the, radicals will not stop trying so we must stop them or suffer for our lethargic stance.

We did win but we cannot let our guard down. The world is in turmoil as I write this with two different beliefs in a battle. That we must win! The price of losing is too great to imagine, I for one do not want my children or grandchildren to have to suffer for our lax ways.

At this time I'm 6 years old, and have just started the first grade, we walk about 1 ½ miles to school. We each have chores to do; if we do not grow our food we go hungry. The Depression is still going strong. The push to produce massive amounts of war material is, just now getting under way. It takes time to change from an industrial to, a war-time machine the, automotive companies must be retooled. Along with all other industries to make Tanks, Jeeps, Trucks, Bombs and the other materials required to fight a war. The fact that people will start to be employed to, meet the needs of the war effort does not eliminate the need to, produce food for the table, or lighten the work load instead it, increases the work load. Each individual must do more, because many of the men are going to fight the war. We still do not have power, running water, refrigeration, or machinery to do our work it, must be done by hand. As my mother and we children walk our cattle the 1 mile to the pasture we are starting to experience strange odors. The war has permeated the air with, smells of burning gun powder, and stench of decay from, the bodies of the dead. This would worsen as the war intensifies.

The year is 1942 one of my older brothers lies about his age to join the Navy. He becomes a frogman he, is 17 years old at the time. March 12th the Philippines are falling to the axis, General McArthur is ordered to leave the island. He vows, "I will return." March 3rd, the U. S. interns 100,000 Americans of Japanese descent. March 28th, the British start making heavy raids on German cities from the air. April 17th, the French General Giraud is captured by the Germans and escapes. Hitler is furious he, states this man by himself is worth 30 divisions. April 9th, most of the 36,000 Americans and Filipino forces on Bataan were killed by an overwhelming force of 200,000 Japanese. April 5th, the British carrier Herms is sunk by Japanese bombs. April 29th, Nazis launch blitzkrieg raids on York, England 5. German planes are shot down by the RAF planes. May 8th, the Japanese are dealt their first heavy blow by the American Navy proving that they are not invincible. May 31st, the Soviet forces slaughter about 90,000 German soldiers on the Kharkov battle front. The Soviet losses are at about 75,000. May 6th, after 300 air raids the American and Filipino troops give in to the Japanese. The Japanese have captured about 42,000 of the American and Filipino troops. May 30th, the RAF put almost every plane it had in the air to raid Cologne, dropping more than 2,000 tons of bombs. The RAF figures it did more damage in this raid than in 1,300 previous raids. They damaged more then 200 factories.

June 7[th,] the battle of Midway is started, after 4 days of savage fighting on the sea, and in the air. The Japanese are forced to withdraw from the fighting. With two or three aircraft carriers and a dozen other ships lost. This is a turning point in the war. June 25th, the American General Eisenhower takes charge in Europe. His job is to coordinate American and British forces. June 25th, the German General Rommel overruns Libya, and leads German forces into Egypt. Rommel is known as the Desert Fox because of his effectiveness in desert fighting. July 28th, the Germans capture Russia's great Black sea naval base at Sevastopol. The Germans pay a high price for the effort they, lost 300,000 troops in the battle. July 16th, the French round up 13,000 Jews with, the Nazis, claiming that doing this will save their lives. The agreement was that the Germans would not deport any French Jews if, the French arrested any Foreign Jews. The French are claiming this move will save many lives; the take is the French made a deal with Hitler-the Devil.

The FBI has rounded up 158 more Germans in the U.S.A. when they cracked down on spies, and saboteurs. August 7th, the U.S. has attacked Guadalcanal. This is a move to seize an airport. This will allow our planes to operate from a closer position to Japan. Thousands of Canadians die as the attack on Dieppe France fails. The hope was that they would learn a way to invade France, and find a way to remove the German occupiers. August 17th, Churchill, U.S. envoy William Averell Harriman and Stalin discuss war plans in Moscow. Sept. 17th, the Germans have reached Stalingrad and Stalingrad is on fire from the German bombing, and ground attack. Sept .12th, a German U-boat sinks a ship carrying 1,800 Italian prisoners of war. This upsets the Italians they, are part of the Axis. Here in the U.S.A. everyone has to sacrifice the, war has created shortages of almost everything. All items required for the war effort are rationed.

Sept. 25th, the U.S. has built 488 ships in one year the, ships are called Liberty ships. The U.S. is using an assembly line method of ship building. The

Germans have executed over 200,000 poor souls up to this time; most of them in Poland. October 31st, General Montgomery takes charge of the British 8th Army, he and Rommel-The Desert Fox prepare for a showdown in Egypt. The Desert Fox is not too optimistic about the outcome. 50 German airplanes made the biggest daytime raid on England since the start of the war. November 11th, in just four days, American forces under the command of General Eisenhower have control of French Africa. The tide is turning step by step. Eisenhower made it clear we are at war with Germany, and Italy, not France. He states "we come among you to remove the invader not, to occupy your land." Nov. 27th, the French destroy most of their largest ships. When the Germans move in to occupy Toulon, a harbor where the ships had taken refuge. The ships are on fire as the Germans move in. This move is a normal act during a war. It removes the ships from service. This way the enemy cannot use them against you or your allies. November 4^{th,} the British 8th Army rout Rommel-The Desert Fox from Egypt capturing at least 9,000 Axis troops in the process.

Nov. 25th, the Russians encircle the Germans at Stalingrad. The tide is being turned on the Russian front many, Germans are being shot in the back when they try to retreat. Many are freezing or starving to death because the supply lines are too long, and the winter is too cold for their clothing. December 2nd, atomic fission is tested. Scientists built a nuclear pile at the University of Chicago. At 3:35 the scientists removed the control rods from the pile, to show the chain reaction process works. This effort is part of the secret Manhattan project, and part of an effort to build an Atomic bomb. Dec.1st, gas rationing is put in place, the gas, and rubber tires are needed for the war effort. Dec. 8th, General Montgomery has Rommel-The Desert Fox on the run.

The year is 1943. January 31st, the German occupiers of Stalingrad are starving, freezing, and out of ammunition. They surrender to the Russians. The fighting was so intense that the, Germans could not reach the supplies that were parachuted to them. The French, the Americans, and the British hold a war council in Casablanca. They agree that peace can only come to the world, after the German and Japanese war powers are completely eliminated. Jan. 30th Berlin is bombed during a bright sunny day. The tide in the war is turning. Jan.5th, renowned Negro educator George Washington Carver has died in Tuskegee, Alabama. He was born a slave in Missouri in 1861. He was a graduate of Iowa State College. Feb. 9th, the Russians are on the move against the Germans and take back Kursk. Feb. 21st, canned food and shoes are rationed in the U.S. they are needed for the troops. Feb. 9th, the Americans are on the move against the Japanese. We are retaking some of the islands from the Japanese.

Feb. 26th, the Americans are on the move against the Germans, Rommel the Desert Fox is surrounded. March 10th Rommel is defeated in Africa and goes back to Europe Ill and exhausted. Adolph Hitler's words are still ringing in his ears. To your troops Hitler said "you can show them no other road than that to victory or death." March 5th, the U.S. planes sink 22 Japanese ships, and 55 Japanese Fighter planes have been shot down. With about 15,000 Japanese troops aboard the ships killed.

April 19th, the Jews in Warsaw, Poland are in a desperate fight to the death. They know that if they do not die in their homes. They will die in the infamous gas chambers, or at a concentration camp. May 27th, the C.I.O. union strikes at Goodyear, Goodrich, General tire and Firestone. President Roosevelt ended the strikes by Presidential decree. May 12th, 150,000 Africa Corps troops surrender to the British General Montgomery. They are battered and worn down. May 17th, the British are bombing the Germans with abandon. They destroy many of the German factories, and break two major dams destroying power stations and flooding many key areas. May 16th, the Germans have killed or captured all Jews in the battle in Warsaw, Poland, they killed more than 56,000. June 1st, Leslie Howard, who played Ashley Wilkes in, *Gone with the Wind,* is killed. The plane he was aboard was shot down, by the Germans. June 22nd, National Guard troops are called in to stop a race riot in Detroit, 29 are killed, and many injured. June 23rd, Allies enter Sicily and capture Palermo. The German troops had withdrawn earlier, and the Italian troops were waiting to surrender. This is the first of many steps in, the process to liberate Europe.

July 13th, the Russians defeat the Germans south of Moscow. Adolph Hitler did not surrender, but he did call it quits. His soldiers and his brand new tanks were defeated. July 25th, Italy, Mussolini is arrested, he acts confused due to the defeat of his nation. The U.S. bombers hit Hamburg, Germany killing some 30,000, and destroying the city. When the bombing was finished all that was left was a pile of bricks. August 18th, the British bomb a secret German weapons base that produces new planes. They are propelled by air rushing through their engines (these are the first jet propelled aircraft). Some of them are called flying bombs (these are the first rockets) and it is noted they do not require pilots.

Sept. 26th, the Russians are defeating the Germans. The Germans have made the mistake of spreading their resources too thin, and cannot supply their troops. Sept. 12th, American and German troops are involved in a furious battle in the Naples area. The British enter the battle from another direction to cut off supplies. The Italians surrender unconditionally, and they turn their ships over to the Allies. Oct. 4th, French Corsica is liberated, this removes a strategic port. The Germans were using to launch U-boat attacks against the Allies. Nov. 29th, Yugoslavia enters the fight helping the British fight the Germans. Nov. 28th, the big three consisting of Stalin, Roosevelt and Churchill, meet in Tehran, discussing plans for the liberation of Europe. Nov. 24th, the U.S. takes the Gilbert Islands after fierce fighting with the Japanese. Dec. 24th, General Eisenhower takes over the northern and western invasions of Europe. Dec.6th, the big three agreed on a plan to subdue the Reich. Dec.31st, the biggest American air fleet hits German targets. They wipe out many important German factories needed by the, Germans to support their war effort.

The year is 1944 and on Jan 20th, the RAF dropped 2,300 tons of bombs on Berlin. Just one week after

1,400 American planes wiped out three Nazi aircraft assembly plants. Jan. 27th, the U.S. has revealed that thousands of American troops were tortured, to death by the Japanese. Jan. 29th, the Germans plan to allow only the perfect Aryan elite people to breed. This is a move to purify the German race. Feb. 15th bombers blast the Nazis at, the fortress of Monte Casino. Allied troops watching the raid from below cheer them on. Feb. 21st, a two day American air offensive with over 2,000 U.S. bombers involved struck eight German plane plants. Destroying over 25% of the Nazi fighter plane plants output. Feb. 29th, General Mac Arthur begins the drive to recover the Pacific Islands. Aerial bombardment is ravaging the Japanese the, price in American lives is heavy.

March 29th, Hungary's Jews are sent to the German gas chambers in Auschwitz as the Russian army approaches. March 8th, the Spitfire is the heroic fighter plane of the war it, devastates the German fighter planes. This causes the Germans to change their invasion plans of Britain. March 26th, the Germans wipe out the French resistance but it, took over 1,000 Germans to do the job. There were only 200 French resistance fighters. March 4th, U.S. planes bomb Berlin for the first time with B-17 bombers, the raid underscores the German vulnerability. March 24th, the German Gestapo executes Italian priests, Jews, Women, and several 14 year old boys. Adolph Hitler demands that 50 Italians be, executed for every German who dies. April 9th, General De Gaulle is named Commander-in-Chief of free French forces. The French are disputing how to manage their part of the Allied invasion of

Western Europe. His job is to get all to cooperate, and organize the invasion effort of the French forces. April 13th, the Russians are on the move. They retake the Kerch Peninsula from the Germans, who took it from the Russians two years ago. April 24th, Allies launch a major offensive in the Netherlands, and New Guinea. They bypass several Japanese strongholds to, gain the more strategic Islands. April 16th, the French that have been serving with the Nazis since, one month after the Germans invaded Russia meet in Paris. At the meeting they were shown a drone that the Germans have developed. April 6th, the Reich is heavily bombed. The Allies have increased the accuracy of their bombing. Now they control the skies over Germany. April 3rd, the courts grant Negroes the right to vote; this causes concern. Southern members of congress are worried about it being extended to, other southern states. May 9th, the Russians free the Crimea. One General was stripped of his rank when, he asked Hitler for permission to surrender.

May 26th, a rumor of women taking off their veils in Syria causes a riot. May 28th, the Allies team up in Italy and menace Rome when they move to take over the country, from the Italians. June 22nd, Roosevelt signs the G.I. bill of rights. This will give veterans $20.00 a week unemployment, a 50% guarantee of loans up to $2,000.00, and grant of up to $500.00 for, four years of training and education. June 4th, Allied forces enter and take over Rome Italy with very little opposition. June 10th, the German SS massacres 642 people in the small French town of Oradour. They kill everyone in sight: women, children, and men down to the last person. June 15th, the U.S. bombs the Island of Kyushu, Japan with B-29 bombers. It is felt that it will not be too long before, Tokyo is next to be bombed. June 6th, D-Day has arrived, the Allies land in great strength in Normandy. Our paratroopers are dropped behind enemy lines. The invasion is successful but the price is high. Freedom must always be paid for in blood and sweat. June 12th, the first V-1 rocket hits London. This is the first of Hitler's new miracle weapons, the missile is jet-propelled, and needs no pilot. It can carry a ton of explosives, and it flies at speeds of up to 370 miles per hour. July 6th, 2,752 people are killed in Britain. The, V-1 flying bombs seem unstoppable. The Nazis are calling it the vengeance rocket. July 31st, the Allied advance in north France, this should soon put them in a position to, move to the German homeland.

July 21st, Truman is Roosevelt's running mate. Roosevelt goes for a fourth term as president. July 20th, the Russians are moving on the Eastern front as Bombs hit Warsaw. The Polish partisans are attacking the Germans from the

Rear. The Russians are hitting the Germans hard this forces them to retreat into the Polish lines. 57,000 Germans march through the streets of Moscow, not as conquerors but as prisoners of war. There is no question that the tide has turned in Eastern Europe. July 20th, Hitler escapes an attack when his secret headquarters was bombed. One of his aids was killed, 12 were injured. Hitler rages about an assassination attempt by an officer's clique he believes was headed by Col. Count Von Stauffenberg. Hitler announced that the Col. was dead. Hitler had him executed. July 22nd, a 44 member International monetary conference was held. The International Monetary Fund is established. By the way this is the start of the International welfare system. The U.S. is the country that underwrites the system. Many countries will default on their loans at our expense. August 8th, Hitler found out about a plot to kill him, and the plotters are hanged. August 25th, French tanks lead the Allies into Paris. The French sing the "Marseillaise." General Charles De Gaulle leads the parade. Aug. 29th, Allies land in southern France. It is noted that if the invasion of Normandy would have been, this easy. Southern France would have been liberated, and the war would be over by now.

Aug. 27th, mass killings of prisoners in Nazi camps are disclosed. The Polish and Russian officials estimate that 1,500,000 Jews and Christians were killed by the Nazis. Aug. 31st, the Russians sweep through Rumania, capturing the oil fields at Ploesti. This is a major slap in the face for the Nazis this was their major supply of oil. This will cripple their war effort. Aug. 31st, as the Russians advance on Warsaw, the Polish underground army warns his government in London. It is said that if the Russians are allowed to take over Poland, they would just be another oppressor. Sept. 8th, the Nazis have a new remote controlled rocket that they are using to hit London. It is called the V-2. The V-2 carries a ton of explosives just like the V-1 did except the V-2 travels faster then than the speed of sound. Because of the speed it is impossible to detect. September 9th, some Belgian cities are liberated by the American forces.

Sept. 15th, the Americans break through into the Reich. Sept. 19th, A Soviet push scares off German Allies. The Bulgarians are intimidated by the recent Russian advances in Eastern Europe, break their ties with the Nazis, and form a new Communist government. Sept. 27th, Allies try to seize a Dutch bridge. Thousands of British, Polish, American, and Dutch soldiers are killed in the attempt. Only 50 of 3,000 paratroopers survived, 10,000 Dutch resistance fighters died; American and British casualties were extremely high also. Sept. 16th, Roosevelt, and Winston Churchill shift the focus of the war effort. To the Pacific, they feel that the Nazis are about finished. October 9th, the big four consisting of the U.S., Great Britain, China and Russia propose that a security organization be formed. The proposed international group will be called the United Nations. The idea is that the big four would attack, any potential war-making country before, rather than after, war is made. The group would use any and all means at their disposal, to maintain or restore peace. What a joke that turned out to be, the U.N. is an organization of greedy, self-serving, do nothing procrastinators. To find out if what is being said is true, all one needs to do is look at their track record. It stinks!

Oct 25th, General MacArthur fulfills his promise; he has returned to the Philippines. With 225,000 men destroying two divisions of the Japanese fleet, the only serious loss is the carrier USS Princeton. It was badly damaged by Japanese bombers. Rather than give the Japanese the satisfaction of sinking it, the U.S. forces torpedoed it. Casualties were very light, all on board were removed. Oct.20th, Allies take the first city in Germany. They dispatch a "surrender or die" ultimatum to the Germans. Oct.14th, Rommel, a hero of the Reich, but an enemy of Hitler died a victim of suicide. He was implicated in the assassination attempt on Hitler. He was offered a choice: commit suicide and be given a hero's burial, or be shot and be disgraced. He chose to swallow the poison pill. Oct 22nd, the Russians entered Prussia, the French prisoners were afraid of their liberators because the Russians are brutal to everyone.

Nov 3rd, there was a grim struggle to open Antwerp to Allied shipping. British and Canadians have taken charge of the area. The German's surrender; now the area can be cleared of the German land mines. Nov. 7th, Roosevelt wins his fourth term as president of the U.S; he defeated Dewey. Nov.12th, the great German battleship, the Tirpitz that has been a menace to Allied shipping is sunk. The RAF bombers do their job. Nov 24th, General Patton's tanks drive into the Saar basin. Capturing the second most important mining and factory region, that has been most essential to the Germans. Dec. 16th, German troops took the Allies by surprise when they, launched a counter-attack in Ardennes. Hitler hopes to reverse his recent setbacks in Belgium and France. Dec. 29th, "Nuts to you" or just plain "Nuts" has become the rallying cry. McAuliffe gives a one word reply "Nuts" to the Germans when he was surrounded, by five German divisions, in the city of Bastogne. The Germans felt he could hold out no longer, supplies could not be gotten to him because, of a snow storm, and the cloud cover.

Several day's later infantry, and armored divisions reached him. Overpowering the Germans and rescuing him. His comment was "I'm happy to see you" there was no doubt that he was very relieved to see the American troops. Dec.5th, a new rank of five Star General has been created in, a unanimous vote by the senate. Immediately after the bills passage four generals get the five star rating; they are George Marshall, Douglas McArthur, Dwight Eisenhower and Henry Arnold. The promotions were to reward these men for the dedication of their lives to the protection of our nation.

The year is 1945 and a very eventful year. The tide has turned on both fronts in the Allies favor. The Germans and Japanese are on the run. I remember these events. Two of my brothers are involved in the 2nd World War so our family follows what, is happening very closely. Jan. 28th, the Japanese are on the run in Burma. The American forces are pushing the, Japanese forces into a position to trap them. The Chinese are closing in from the opposite direction. They need to clear the New Ledo and Burmese roads for use. Before, the road can be used the retreating Japanese forces must be removed. Jan. 27th, Auschwitz is liberated when the Soviet troops sweep through Poland. When the soldiers walk through the barbed wire of the Auschwitz concentration camp, they discover 5,000 prisoners. Most of them are Jews, all of them dazed, and starving. These prisoners were the lucky ones. Thousands were asphyxiated in the gas chambers of Auschwitz by the Nazi. They were intent on purifying the German race. Jan. 31st, the Soviet army is battering Berlin's outer defenses they, capture the town of Beyersdorf. The Nazi broadcasts express fears that, the Russians are prepared to, launch a frontal attack on Berlin.

Jan. 18th, Churchill warns the Reich to surrender he states that Germany has less to fear in surrendering unconditionally, than in continuing a hopeless war. Feb.11th, the big three plan future moves in Europe about, how to split up the conquered countries. Russia had such resounding victories Stalin was negotiating from a position of strength. He could not be denied control of the countries Russia conquered. Russia ended up with control of most of Europe. The U.S. was intent on devoting most of its energy on Japan. To Roosevelt the Russians were invincible. They swept through Eastern Europe into Western Europe with ease. The Allies were stumbling, and Germany was in ruins. The French were a mess, disorganized, and the British were overloaded.

Feb.14th, Dresden, which is Germany's gem, is devastated. Allied planes bombed the city for two weeks. More than 130,000 people were killed, mostly civilians. For most of the war Dresden was left alone, it was not an industrial city but of historical value. Now all bets were off the table, there were no safe places, in Germany. Feb.17th, U.S. forces liberate Manila, and find 5,000 POW's there. Feb. 25th, B-29's bomb Tokyo over, and over dropping 2,000 tons of bombs on its industrial sections. Tokyo is in disarray, and there is no letup in the bombing. Feb. 23rd, after four days of bitter fighting the Stars and Strips are raised over the island of Iwo Jima. The Japanese are overcome by the

U.S. Marines. March 25th, German teenagers calling themselves the Werewolves, assassinate the Mayor of Aachen. The Mayor was an American appointee. March 8th, the American forces crossed the Rhine for the first time since, the war began, and discover another bridge intact. The Germans in their haste to retreat forgot to blow it up; it was a railway bridge.

March 6th, the Communists take charge in the Balkans. Many of the countries seem to favor the Soviet form of government. So they are falling into the Communist rule. April 12th, Roosevelt dies, the war is about to come to an end. He died of a cerebral hemorrhage; he was at his retreat in Warm Springs, Georgia, resting up. His death came at a time of high triumph. All under his command were at the gates of Berlin, and the shores of Japan with victory in sight. April 12th, Harry S. Truman becomes the President of the U.S; he had served just a few months as Vice President when Roosevelt died, making him the President. April 13th, Vienna is in the Red Russian armies' grasp.

April 15th, 2,000 pieces of art work are found. They were stolen by the Nazis, and stored in a German iron mine. The newly formed United Nations meet to organize. All nations are asked to rise above their personal interest for the, good of the world (by the way it still has not happened). April 27th, the Ukrainian and American forces join up in the heartland of Germany. Their forces split Germany into two defeated parts. Now all of Germany is under Allied control. April 28th, the Father of Italian Fascism is put in front of a firing squad, when he and 11 others are convicted of war crimes after a quick trial. He cries "let me live, let me live I will give you an empire." April 30th, Hitler commits suicide as Russian troops move in. He shoots his mistress Eva Braun and then himself. Their bodies were set on fire outside their bunker.

The man Adolph Hitler, most Germans would salute as Mein Fuher, died a coward, by taking his own life. As the American soldiers entered the Buchenwald concentration camp they. Were greeted by, the almost dead the prisoners were in such horrible shape. They could hardly lift their heads to look at their liberators. Many of them had Maggots in the corners of their sunken eye sockets. Their muscles were eaten away, a result of starvation. Hitler killed approximately 9 million poor souls in his concentration camps. About 2 million were Jews. In this instance the soldiers were walking where 50,000 innocent souls had met their deaths. This is a result of, the complacency of the peoples of the world. Hitler's horror stories of his demented beliefs unfolded. April 30th, the Russians enter Berlin, Germany gasps its last breath before defeat. May 7th, the Germans surrender unconditionally, and Europe wakes up to freedom. May 23rd, the third Reich dissolves, and died this day. The leaders either escape or take the poison pill. The cowards commit suicide.

May 23rd, Churchill resigns and calls for elections. Britain will hold its first general election in 10 years. June 7th, the German citizens are forced to view a film about the horrors of the Third Reich. Some expressed disbelief, expressing doubt that the Germans were responsible. Some others wept openly, some had no doubt about what took place. The well-fed SS women were forced to bury the corpses of prisoners who starved to death. June 21st, the battle for Okinawa is the bloodiest battle of the pacific so far. The Americans have the victory. The Japanese have lost over 100,000 lives. June 5th, Germany is divided into four zones each, of four nations will occupy a zone. June 21st, Moscow, Joseph Stalin has formed a new regime for Poland. The Polish now are under communist rule. June 23rd, Simon Lake, the person who invented the sub dies at age 78. Now that Europe is under control. American forces can concentrate their efforts on the Japanese-Far East front. June 26th, there is a lot of tension between Russia and the western Allies; all of the differences that were ignored during the fighting rear their ugly heads, when Stalin demands a greater share of Germany. Russia swept through Europe with such ease that the allies fear her.

The Allies demand Japan surrender or she will lay herself open to "complete and utter destruction." The U. S. already has started to attack the Japanese homeland. June 26th, the United Nations is officially formed. Truman, the U.S. president, says, "Oh, what a great day this can be in history." 50 nations are involved in the meeting. The new charter provides what the framers hope will be a new start on, the way to a lasting peace. We all know by now the U.N. is a gutless organization, at best. July 1st, now that the war has ended the wartime partners divide up Germany, and begin the occupation.

In August the Atomic bomb that the U. S. started to develop in 1939 at a cost of 2 billion dollars is operational. The first bomb was dropped on Hiroshima,

Japan on August 6th, Monday at 9:15 a.m. by a Super-fortress named the Enola Gay (the pilot's mother's name) the pilot's name was Col. Paul W Tibbets Jr. The Hiroshima weapon is said to have more power than 20,000 tons of TNT. This is 1,000 times more powerful than the most powerful conventional weapon. Those who flew the mission said that there was a bright flash then, churning debris rose 1000 feet off the ground with a cloud of white smoke that climbed to 20,000 feet, and looked like a mushroom. The reconnaissance flights show that the bomb wiped out over 4 square miles of Hiroshima, or 60 % of the city. A second bomb was dropped on Nagasaki, on August 9th, after president Truman warned the Japanese that the first weapon was a warning of things to come, if they did not surrender. The Japanese offer to surrender came shortly after, the second bomb was dropped. They describe the weapon as inhumane. They ignore what they forced upon our troops with the Bataan death march, among other things equally deplorable. August 15th, 1945, the 2nd World War is ended, the Japanese surrender. The United States gives peace a hearty welcome, after the long awaited victory over Japan; the celebration is called the V-J Day.

No more war, for now. August 14th France's Marshal Petain who led many Frenchmen astray is found guilty of helping the enemy. He passed information to the Germans. August 31st, the secret is out, three hidden cities were built to produce the Atomic bomb. The people that lived, and worked in those cities did not know what they were building. They were all were doing small parts of a big puzzle. The location of the city was Los Alamos, 30 miles north of Santa Fe, New Mexico. Ho Chi Minh is the Communist master of Vietnam. He led the Communist guerrillas of Vietnam in the fight against the Japanese. September 2nd, 1945 Japan officially signs the, unconditional surrender agreement on the American battleship, the Missouri. General MacArthur who accepted the Japanese surrender said, "It is my hope that from this solemn occasion a better world shall emerge out of the blood, and carnage of the past." We all know that it did not happen the, world is still mired in a struggle to find peace. With the U.N. being part of the problem, too much time is wasted talking, trying to find a diplomatic solution. Most countries on the U.N. council want to serve their own purpose, not for the good of all like intended. Sept. 8th, Korea is divided at the 38th parallel. The Americans occupy the south and the Soviets the north. They state it is the intent to make Korea one again. Again we all know it did not happen, the U.N. was involved in that mess. Sept. 5th, the truth is out the Japanese have tortured, starved, beat, shot, and set afire many thousands of American prisoners. Sept. 21st, the British promise India their independence from colonial rule. There are demands that Burma, Malaya, Indochina and the Indonesian islands be freed from imperialist domination.

Sept. 21st, Henry Ford, Jr. takes over Ford Motor Co. from his grandfather. All production is halted and 50,000 workers were laid off. The U.A.W. calls many strikes warning that, it may get worse if their demands are not met. Sept. 24th, General Hideki Tojo, premiere of Japan at the time of the attack on Pearl

Harbor, tries to commit suicide. General Mac Arthur orders the arrest of Tojo's entire cabinet. The turmoil continues there, is a power struggle amidst the various factions of the world powers. October 20th, the Middle East has its own conflicts in the Arab states. They form the Arab league consisting of Egypt, Syria, Iraq and Lebanon warning, that if a Jewish state is formed in Palestine, there would be war. So much for the war that just ended, "ending all wars." I have studied the Arab countries as a youngster. They are fierce warriors, and have been fighting amongst themselves forever. Do you think anyone can stop them now, and how? Oct. 23rd, the first Negro baseball player is hired for the Major Leagues. His name is Jack Roosevelt Robinson. He joined the Brooklyn Dodgers; what a great one he turned out to be. Oct. 24th, the traitors are being caught. Pierre Laval of France and Vidkun Abraham Quisling of Norway are executed, for aiding the Germans.

The reason I have chronicled the events of this time, is to illustrate that we are in the same situation we, were before the 2nd World War. If one looks, and listens to the rants of various world leaders, watch's the maneuvering of others. You can see that, before the 2nd World War we had, Hitler talking peace while preparing for war, in his fantasy of creating the perfect, Aryan blue-eyed, blond-haired race of people. All the while everyone thought they could talk to him. They felt he was reasonable, or would be, or we could just ignore him, and everything would be all right. Today radical Islamists are calling for the death of Israel, and all people of the world that do not believe like they do. They will stop at nothing, including strapping on a belt loaded with explosives, and blow themselves up to gain what they believe is right. The countries of the world, and many of the people in America want to talk, they believe if we talk to them, everything will be alright.

What is different then, it was before the 2nd world war? Not much, China is building a robust war machine, Russia has a leader that is manipulative with the, "if you trust me I will kill you smile" (you fool). France and Germany take the attitude that we can talk to them, and everything will be alright. While all this manipulating is going on. We have Russia, Germany, France, China, North Korea and God only knows, what other countries supplying war materials, and technology to the fanatics of our time. The U.N. is a useless piece of garbage. It does nothing but talk. If one were to look at the U.N.'s record it is a do-nothing, extremely expensive, self-serving bunch of crooks. That aids the cause of the radicals by their peacenik (liberal) attitude. All one need do is watch the rants of the various leaders of Iran, Syria, Venezuela. The way Russia, Germany, France and China use the U.N. to block any activity. That would help force the nations that are causing problems, to step back in line. If you listen while they are talking, you will hear the same ranting, and all of the lies that preceded the 2nd World War. They talk peace while gearing up for war. The fools (liberals) and others will believe them and do nothing. To stop them because they believe talk will solve all problems. Think about this for a minute, we are in Iraqi because the U.N. did not act on, the referendums that were passed. They promised Iraqi if they did not cooperate there would be, impending military action against them. I believe there were 18–19 referendums without action. So much for the preemptive action to prevent war that the U.N. states in its charter the, reason it was founded.

Now in defense of the liberals and the twisted thinking they have, we also have the conservatives that are not any different. If we look at what is being said here we, have a dysfunctional group running the country. The crux of it is that both the Democrats and the Republicans do the same wrong things for the country. But each has their own unique demented twist as to how it should be done. The Constitution says "by the people for the people" not "by a few for the majority." Also it does not say by "self-serving crooks and thieves" like is taking place. Our government is only supposed to do the things that, we and the states cannot do. The government's main purpose is to protect us from external conflicts. Let us take a look at a scenario that sets up a business to, operate like the U. S. government does. With leaders, and workers that have no sense of fiscal responsibility. They do not make good decisions. Do not show up for work about 50% of the time. Have credit cards with no limits. Do nothing when they do show up for work. *Oh My God* I just described our Senate and Congress.

We cannot run a business this way, and the U.S. government is the largest business in the world. It is failing! So what do we do? The solution is simple but painful. The fools we let run our affairs have us in a world of hurt. We must get back to basics. What is

meant by saying get back to basics? We will number
the things we need to do to, turn the corner, so the
U.S. can get its head out of the clouds, and its feet on
the ground. Granted these things will be radical by
political standards, and painful, to say the least. Here
we go: # 1) Show up for work; # 2) Apply common
sense to all decisions; # 3) Be honest above all else; #
4) Do what the people want you to; # 5) Do not allow
a Judge or a Lawyer to overrule the people, the majority rules "by the people for the people." Not by a few
for many. # 6) Do not try to support the world, It is
not our job; # 7) Do not support an organization that
does not accomplish anything (the U.N.). Or give our
resources (money) to a country that does not give in
return; # 8) Review all welfare rolls, only about 15 %
of those who get it do deserve it (real welfare reform).
Put the rest of them to work. # 9) Let the people you
work for decide if you get a raise. You must obey the
law, and be policed by someone other than yourself; #
10) Outlaw all lobbying (you work for the people) so
serve them, not someone else.

Return the pledge of allegiance and the 10
Commandments to our schools, courts, and our life so
our children have a code of ethics that they, can believe
in. That will lead them down a path that is, good for
all. You need to adhere to a set of rules that keep you
on a path that is, good for the country. Just remember
rule # 1, # 2 and # 3 are the first steps. When in doubt
apply # 2 very generously, it covers all situations. Let
us start to work toward where every morning, before
school classes start our, children recite the pledge of
allegiance to our flag. This way our children will be

taught what the U.S. is all about, and have a devotion to something good. Last, but not least, our country was founded by a group of people that wanted religious freedom (God-fearing people). So let's include the basis of our founding fathers back, into the U.S. because without a belief or a dream the people perish. Our kids need something to believe in that is real, Hollywood is not, and it is a bad influence for them, because 95% of what they, produce is trash.

We, the people need to hold our legal system, and our leaders to a higher standard. They do not answer to anyone but themselves. They are not expecting much of themselves. If you want proof of what is being said just take a look, you will see the pork barrel projects that, do nothing but waste our tax dollars. What needs to happen is this: we, the people need to handle the budgets of, our elected officials for one year. At the end of the year their budget would be returned to them. We would return it to them in same condition they have, the Federal government in. They would understand how we feel about, how well they are taking care of our money. I feel that there is no way that bunch of Knuckleheads in Washington will do anything. Until we cause them to! They do not have enough common sense to, pour pee out of a boot with the, directions written on the heel. If you do not believe this just take a look at, what has happened, with the smoke and mirrors tricks they all have pulled. Balancing the budget, passing laws, and the handling of problems of any kind. With how they address issues with other countries, and any other situations that have come up, the grade is F-. I'm being generous! I feel the job they have done is worse than the F-. We have not had good leadership in Washington for so long that it is pathetic. They are all a bunch of **Crooks!** If that group in Washington were asked to join the procrastinators club, they would go on vacation or die of old age. If, **God** forbid they did make a decision they would screw it up, like they have done for years.

The irony of all of this is we only get to vote for what is offered by each party. So it is a vote for the lesser of two evils in most elections. A businessman that would run the country like it should be run, does not stand a chance because we, have a two party system. If you put both parties in the same pot, and stirred it up, when you dumped out the mixture you, would not find a recognizable difference that would, allow you to separate the two. You would have a blending of the same thing both, the Democrats and the Republicans are self-serving dogs who could, give a damn about you. This means, most times when there is an election, if we vote for one it is about the same, like voting for the other Candidate each, will manage the country poorly.

Shock and awe in Iraqi. What a joke but typical of what our leadership, Rummy is capable of. Just like Hollywood no real substance. I have studied the Arab countries for years, and if we are **Dumb** enough to think we can change that, vengeful group that have operated that way for time immemorial, in a matter of a few years. We are **Dumber** than a rock. Take a look! They are taught from little on, that if you kill my brother than, I'm duty-bound to kill you. You're family is duty bound to kill the killer. This thinking perpetuates itself until it becomes a way of life. Now let's relate that to our involvement in Iraq. We have killed many Iraqis. Each is duty-bound to get revenge. Now we have an entire country that is duty-bound to kill all of us. Hell they have been doing it to each other for time immemorial. Yes they hate each other but like, the Iranians have stated when asked to help in Iraq "we hate the Americas more and will join forces to kill them."

Do you want to make a bet? Picture this: if they were successful in, killing all of us. They would then turn on each other when they, finished celebrating their victory. There just is no end to this rat race, and the rats are winning. Yes many of the Iraqis would like to have peace. They have been betrayed by the U.S. before, so now they do not trust us? I for one cannot blame them we say, one thing then, do something completely different. Also they have watched us put Saddam in power, to try to balance out the situation with the Iranians when, the Iraqis, and the Iranians were at war. We, in the U.S. (our supposed leaders) have mismanaged things so many times. We try to buy friends-peace with the almighty dollar. We cater to an organization that has worse managers than our group in Washington, the U.N. And we dump more money than any other country into, the support of that irrelevant organization. In fact we are fools for trying to buy friends. We contribute about 1/3 of the total support of that misfit organization.

We only get one vote. If we use good sense we would do a proportional contribution. We would contribute an amount equal, to all other countries that get a vote. Using *Common* sense it would tell you-anyone that is the only fair thing to do. Then the likes of Kooky Annan would have less to mismanage-steal. This happened with the oil for food program. My question is when do we stop the officials in Washington, from using the people's money-tax dollars, to do such *dumb* things? It reminds me of the movie *Dumb* & *Dumber.* Of course one must realize that the politicians in Washington, police themselves, so what do, we expect? They believe they are above the law, this happens time, and time again when they are caught cheating.

One of the real big problems remains a, *Lobbyist* waving lots of cash in front of them. Of course these Knuckleheads have their hand out, peddling the influence they have, being a Congress person or a Senator in Washington. Basically they sell us down the tube because of their *Greed.* Then in turn investigate themselves; what a joke they are. Can you imagine private industry being run this way, yes it happens but when they are, caught (if they do not buy their way out) they go to jail. This should happen to the *Jerks* in Washington, when they are caught. What a mess! So now that we know about these things, what are we going to do? Vote for the dishonest power brokers they place on the ballot? This is no way to solve the problem? We must find a way, they will not. The only way I know that will work, is to make them uncomfortable every day until, they perform.

Let's take a look at our legal system, and how much meaning our laws have today. Let's start with the basics, so we establish a basis for what is being said. Looking at the basics, I feel we must start with the speed limits placed on our highways. They carry about as much meaning as most of our other laws. Unless you break the speed limit by some astronomical number or there is a speed trap setup. To satisfy some power- happy law enforcement group that wants to create a source of, funding for some reason. It is not uncommon to see cars, and trucks going 30–40 MPH over the speed limit. Why bother to spend the money-resources to put up signs that don't mean a darn thing? Does 55 MPH mean 55 MPH? Or does it mean you can go any speed you want? From where I sit it means you can go any speed you want. Unless you have a police officer that wants to do a good job (there are some of those you know). Or a police officer that wants to go on an ego trip. To prove he-she can control what you do, on what they consider their highway. Does this happen? It sure does. I have had police officers that were in unmarked cars try to control traffic, by playing what I call the 49–57 game (they go 57 miles per hour then slow to 49 to, see if you will pass them). I have put my speed control on at 56–57. When they would drop back to the 49 part of the game, I would ease by them in defiance of their B.S. on two occasions I have had the, officers stop me. Write a ticket, and lie about how fast I was going, go absolutely crazy because I passed them on what they, called their road they stated "no one but no one passes me on my road." Needless to say I took the case to court myself on each occasion. Won each time, I got the officer to reenact his temper tantrum in front of the judge. The net of this is why put up signs that say, the law is one thing. Than make it meaning less by not enforcing the law? I just do not get it!

Going forward now we have established the basis for a deeper, more meaningful discussion. Regarding the disobedience of our laws let's start by reviewing an incident that happened, in 1969. Senator Ted Kennedy was responsible for the death of the, Kopechne girl on July 30th, 1969. Why wasn't there an investigation? Why wasn't he tried? Is Ted above the law? Why was it kept quite? This is a major incident possibly, murder and it just kind of faded off into the sunset like, nothing happened. Why? I think all of us know the answer to these questions. I feel Ted got by with murder. We all know what would have happened if one of us had, pulled a stunt like that, don't we?

Now we have another Kennedy that is drunk or on drugs. Gets stopped by the police, but he is a congressman. He claims he is going to make a vote at 1–2 AM? Being a Congressman makes him immune to prosecution? Come on, do they think we just got off of the turnip truck? Oh, but he went to drug-alcohol treatment so it is okay. The treatment trick is often used as a cop-out by politicians when they get caught. Somehow if they do the treatment thing then they feel they are redeemed? Look at what Foley did, when he got caught. He pulled the treatment thing, acting like that justified what he had done, when he, betrayed the trust placed in him. No, it is not Ok. Stick their butts in jail, just as would be done to one of us. Where is the law that is supposed to apply equally to everyone regardless of, means or stature?

Talk about using your position, look at Congressman

Jefferson and the cool move he made. Speaking of cool he was, hiding $90,000.00 in his freezer wasn't that, a cool move on his part? As usual it was dropped, without much noise he is black, and one of our chosen ones, they are above the law. What do these *Jerks* think? We are stupid? Trying to get us to think that, cash just drops out of the sky into their freezer? We need to get rid of the lobbyists—- we need to try these *Crooks*. Just like we would be tried if we had done, what they do. We need to find a way to stop them from, being their own police. Unless this happens they will continue to abuse the trust we, have placed-misplaced in them. These people don't know how to manage our resources, in a reasonable common sense way.

Have passed laws that tell how, to raise children saying we cannot spank them, or discipline them, too harshly. Or what may be considered too harsh, by a social worker that has, no experience raising children. Our leaders and a few misfits are telling the children, there are no consequences for your misbehavior. Then we add the households with no fathers. A stable household with two parents with, a reasonably structured environment equals good kids. I for one hope we know why, we have the problems in our homes and schools. When our kids are not disciplined in the home because, the parents are too lazy, don't give a damn or are too scared of the law to, discipline their kids.

How can one get the message across that if, you do something wrong, you have to suffer the consequences of, your misbehavior? No wonder we have a bunch of lazy kids that don't know the difference, between right and wrong. It is called, the dumbing up of America. They are doing a bang up job of it.

We have too many people in our schools doing too little, too many non-productive-administrative personnel. If a child is too smart or advanced for their age, the teachers do not know how, to handle them, in most cases. They are taught to handle average children, if one is above average they, slip through the cracks. Because most teachers do not know what to do, if a child is below average it is easy, most schools have special classes for them. In many of the cases if a child is somewhat mischievous, like I was, they are placed in the special education class, even if the child is advanced for their age. The special education classes are for, slow learners this is bad news for an above average kid and simply bores them with the slow pace of the lessons. Thank God they did not have special education classes back when, I was going to school. The special education classes provide an easy way out for, teachers that do not know how to cope. This is just another example of how unreasonable, our system has become.

In recent times we have had, demented judges that, leave sexual deviates out of jail. Within weeks or months of being released the, deviate kills a child or woman. We think the judge should serve the same punishment, like the deviate. There must be a consequence for his actions also. Or take the judge that gave the sexual deviate 60 days sentence. We need to castrate the deviate as, a first effort then take, more drastic action if that does not do the job. We have too many deviate men and women, running around loose, we cannot or do not keep track of. We must protect our children from this trash. We must do something to stop the Hollywood trash peddlers with, their sick, kill 'em, screw 'em movies. No wonder we have major problems with our kids. All we have is too many laws that mean nothing. Too many judges that are not, worth a darn, and in many cases may, be deviates themselves. Do not misunderstand what is being said here. We do have some, real super teachers and judges; just that too many are, too lazy to do a good job or, simply not fit to be a judge or a teacher. We need to get back to basics, if we don't we will go, down the tubes. Just like other countries before us have, when they accepted second best, as a way of life because it, was easier, than putting forth the effort to do the, job right.

Laws do not serve a purpose unless they are enforced, this way they mean something, and they must be enforced equally. Most laws are simply a piece of paper that says something, means nothing, because there is no, enforcement of the law as written. A match can take care of a piece of paper in a second, and a law that is not enforced has no more, meaning than that. That's enough about our legal system. We all know that it is *Sick;* now how do we make it well? We, people must demand something happen to, change what is taking place. Because it is obvious that Washington is not going to, do anything, except what they have been doing, which is nothing or worse, pass another meaningless law. What they have been doing is passing laws in layers (in other words they pass a law that is like a law that was passed earlier) that is not enforced. Their mentality is that a piece of paper will solve the problem. Paper does not solve problems, action does these people are too *dumb* to realize that. We cannot expect much out of people that only work part-time, and do nothing, when they do, show up for work. We need to fire them, and replace them with people that want to, straighten this mess out. Hopefully it is not too late.

Ever since the 2nd World War we have had a bunch of welfare, deficit spending fools running the country. The Democrats and the Republicans have tried to outdo, each other in an effort to get their self-serving party elected-reelected. Doesn't any one of them really give a damn about what, happens to the U. S. A.? I cannot believe that this senseless B.S. continues. We have a legal system that. Is meaningless-irrelevant, we have a brainless cycle of, over spending, and waste. This puts us deeper in debt, it just doesn't make sense. No one gives a damn! Things must change! I will defend Ronald Reagan, and Jack Kennedy. They did many good things along with a few other good presidents, it is just that we have had too few worth a damn. The last three were not included in the good one's grouping. Let's take a brief look at the last three, Bush one promised one thing when, campaigning, "read my lips no new taxes." Clinton was all, smoke and mirrors but he is famous for, "I did not have sex with, that women." The present Bush wants to make believe, if you do nothing it will be ok. So he lets the, pork slip through the proverbial cracks. Bush is our President I support him, and support our troops. But this guy cannot manage a business, and the U.S. government is the largest business, in the world. He does not veto the bills that are placed in front of him that, are loaded with wasteful pork. Oh he has vetoed a few lately. But it is too little, too late. We cannot forget the good old peanut farmer. You know! The one with the big mouth that was the worse President we have, ever had. He could not get the job done, and now he runs around saying how, wrong things are. Jimmy Carter is his name. He is the one that started his Presidency with the, attempted rescue of the American hostages. That Iran was, holding in the desert. The rescue attempt was all screwed up. He did not know what to do, so he did nothing. This was the start of Jimmy Carters Presidency, and from here it got worse. Jimmy was not a bad person he was, put in a job he could not handle is all. It happens!

Now let's talk about trade with, other countries. Enter the W.T.O. (Worse Thing Organization) that we have joined. That can tell us if, we restrict the incoming goods from a country that we are wrong. We must accept the goods, or we are labeled protectionists. My question is how, can another group or country tell us, we must allow unlimited products, or for that matter any product from, another country to enter our country? I'm for unlimited free trade. There is one simple rule that would, govern the trade it, is what I call "*Zero* the hero." Any country we trade with could, ship unlimited product to our country. The balance of payments must equal *Zero* at, the end of the year. If it does not, no more product could be shipped until, the balance equaled *Zero* plus 5% or less. Come on now, we cannot keep trying to, give the country away. This has been happening, let's get some common sense in the picture, and make it fair for both parties. Let's stop shipping our, good jobs and technology over seas.

Now we have this group that was appointed, to see what we could do in Iraq, to get a handle on, that mishandled mess. They have come up with some, real wild ideas, such as talk to Iran, and Syria to try to get them to help. The way I would do it is to put a feeler out, to see if in fact they are interested in talking. I would bet that, they would take that like a sign of weakness. It would be a give me what I want one-sided situation, like happened with Clinton, and Israel with the roadmap for peace deal. Palestine was taking but, not giving nothing, and demanding more. Clinton tried to get the Jews to give Israel away. Each time a concession was made to the Palestinians they, would accept the concession, than demand more. When you try to give something, to get something, these people take it, like a sign of weakness. These people are not reasonable people to deal, with unless, it fits their agenda. They will not accept whatever you offer, without further demands. My question is, are our leader's trying to give Israel to the Palestinians? *This is crazy!* You do not lock the fox in the hen house to see, if it will protect the hens. Do you? It still remains if it is good, and you want it screwed up, let Washington handle it. Guess what, it will be screwed up, you can take that to the bank. Enough of that, it is, and remains that we have a Fox, watching the proverbial hen house. I just do not see any light at the end of this tunnel. Something has to change or, the future of America is in jeopardy. We need leaders that really care!

The reason that I have chronicled many of the

events from the 1st World War on is to, illustrate the similarities of events that are, taking place now. Plus many of you do not know about, the events that took place. You were not taught this part of history in school or, not much about it. When I ask the young children of today if they know of Pearl Harbor they, say we, heard something about it. What was it? In one case I asked a 50 year old person if, they knew what Pearl Harbor was all about, and they said "yup I know about Pearl Harbor my, only question is, what did we do to, cause them to attack us at, Pearl Harbor"? Now just like in the roaring 20's we have, credit running rampant. Almost everyone is in hock up to, their eyebrows. We think we can talk to, the likes of North Korea, Syria, Iran, Russia is our friend? China is using us like the dumb butts we are, to finance the build up of their war machine. All the while we are talking peace to them, and are being misled by their talk about, becoming a more open society with more, freedom for their people. Let's take a look at what other countries are using us: Africa, some of South America, most of the Arab countries, Indonesia, Russia, China, France, Germany, Spain, and about every country in the world is, depending on the U.S. market to support them. The U.S. dollar is so inflated, and the federal debt is so large. It amazes me that we can continue to thrive.

Just take a look at how we finance a house for the over-spending younger generation. It is now a pretty common a lack of common sense practice to, loan 125 % of a house's value. A person can buy a house with no down payment, and interest-only loans for, a number of years. Can you imagine what happens when, after 5 years all of a sudden the payment goes to principle, and interest? Say paying the interest only, the payment is $800.00, and with the normal principle-interest payment the, payment is $1,200.00. The folks buying the house have other, debts that consume all their earnings. This causes a shortfall that cannot be covered. Inflation will not, cure our problems, and we cannot just keep turning up the money pump without, causing inflation. We are in a Rat race and the Rats are winning. What really amazes me is how each President will say, like Clinton did, and Bush is doing. The federal government will, not have deficit spending the year after they leave office. The federal debt will be paid off in 10 years. It is all smoke and mirrors, and typical of Washington. What a bunch of liars, if their nose would grow an inch for each lie they told, all of them would have noses, a mile long. So it goes just like it was, back in the roaring 20's. We are being set up by our leaders for, a hard fall. I feel that it is past due so hang on it, will be a rough ride.

We are also being set up for, a major conflict that will devastate the entire world. This happened when Hitler was ranting, and raving about being peaceful. Look around and you will see Iran doing, the Nukes-for-peace thing. The North Koreans have the nuke, and I feel both will share it with, the radicals. If we do our passive thing as, we did in the 1920's and 1930's we can expect the same results. This go around it will be much more devastating. Remember Pearl Harbor the 65th anniversary was December 7th of the year 2006 as the Japanese invaded December 7th, 1941.

We are helping the Russians and the Chinese in every way we can, to finance their military buildup. Allowing them to use our markets or, by giving them foreign aid. Buying friends is not a, lasting way of making peace. We are trying to appease these tyrants, by letting them use the, American markets like they please. We are trying to reason with North Korea with, the 5 party talks, or sanctions on Iran, with Russia and China permanent members of the U.N. with veto power. Plus we have the French, and Germans trying to pacify them by being nice. What a joke this approach is. The irrelevant U.N., the pacifist Knuckleheads, the Russians, and Chinese are playing us like a fiddle. We believe they are selling weapons and technology to the radical groups that rant and rave. With the hope that, we will be weakened where, the U.S.A. is irrelevant. Why would they do this?

The reason they would do this is they are envious of what America "The Great Experiment" has accomplished. Russia is reverting to the socialistic country it was, during the Cold War. A closed society under Putin's rule, everyone will behave, or disappear one, way or another. This has happened with the, nuclear poisoning of several Russian's that did, not agree with the way things are run? Russia is awash with oil, the government owns it. This means they have tons of cash to spend now, and Russia-Putin wants the price of oil to stay high. This way America has less money to spend. The Arab countries want oil to stay high for the same reasons. The oil producing countries are in cahoots with each other. They limit production to keep oil prices high. Why? It is my belief that this is their way of trying to destroy the dollar, the standard of trade world wide. In other words they all want America "The great Experiment" to default at some point.

Take a look at China, an example of a mixture of two conflicting societies. China is a hybrid society with a dominant ruling group, with the freedoms for some people to keep some of what they create. Although it's sure that the ruling group is taking care of their chosen ones. This way they can control the masses. We say that because, about 99 % of the Chinese people are more or less slaves of the (their bosses) state. It is my belief China is also part of the same plot. Why would we say that? China has no interest in anyone but China! All you need to do is look at how abusive China is, when it comes to trade. If, China is interested in a long term trade relationship, they would insist on the trade being fairer. Like it is now, it is one sided. They are only interested in what they can get. To find out if what is said is true. Look at the balance of payments with China, the balance of payments tells the truth, and the balance with China is unhealthy. Another indicator is what, are they doing with the money from the trade? In China's case it sure is not going to the common people. Too much of it is going to a military buildup, to be healthy for the rest of the world. The Chinese have rockets, they have nuclear bombs, and if they do not have delivery capability now, they will have it soon. If we have a conflict with them it will have to be nuclear.

China has too many people to be able to fight them on the ground. China also had-has a program where girl babies were-are aborted. Why? China had-has a plan to have a 100,000,000 man Army, this Army is to be made up of 100,000,000 men with no women to love. An Army with this many angry men would be, an Army larger then all the Armies of the world put together. All 100,000,000 of them angry at, who ever they are told to be angry at. Watch out! This is why they were aborting the girl babies. Recently China reversed the abortion policy because there are, too many men with no women to love. This caused a major problem, because too many of the men were turning Gay. The Chinese are very patient people. If you would like to understand how they think read Sun Tzu the Art of War. It is a good book that will teach you about, how Chinese leaders handle situations. When reading the book you will learn how, to handle situations in your life. Hopefully this discussion about the Chinese will, give you a better understanding of what we are dealing with. Because it should be a major concern, for all of us, from several stand points. Number one the trade balance aspect and two the military aspect.

Hopefully our elected officials will address the trade, and foreign aid situation. With the expectation that, the country receiving the foreign aid become, self- sustaining, within a time frame that is reasonable. A fair trade agreement that is equitable for both parties. Hopefully this will be addressed before it is too late time is running short, just like it did prior to the 2nd World War. What is the solution? The U. S. A. needs to pay attention to the signs of the times. Build up our armed forces so, we are prepared for whatever situation we are confronted with. This way we will not have a repeat of, what took place at Pearl Harbor. This time if, we allow it to happen, because we are not diligent, it will be much worse, like outlined earlier. We cannot afford to screw around like the James Baker group, called the Iraqi commission wants us to do. If we do we have had it! That group, and the pacifist group we now have in Washington have, a screw loose if they think that talking will do the job.

These people understand only one thing they (the various tribes in the Arab world) have been, warring with each other since the beginning of time. They only understand strength-power. Anything less is a joke to them. Guess how they feel about the group in Washington? You got it, they are happy as hell that the, Democrats got in office. This talk group will give them all the time they need, to do their nuke thing. Watch out, the conditions are ripe for the, repeat of the 1920s, 1930s and the 1940s. Just look around you. Aren't most people in hock over their heads? Isn't everyone fat dumb, and happy (Just as Hitler said a chicken in every pot and a Volkswagen in every driveway)? Then you can tell the people anything, and they will believe you. For Hitler this worked, he had the world believing he was peaceful. He talked peace just like many are doing today, (our nukes are for peaceful purposes). Then we have the despot that promises us: hell on earth because, he already has nukes, but cannot deliver them "yet." Keep talking, give him time like we are doing, and the "yet" will disappear. Or worse "yet" he will give or sell them to the wacko fanatics in the Middle East. They will hand deliver them as a dirty bomb. Worse "yet" they will pack them in a shipping container, and ship them over here. Then, detonate them in one or several of our ports at the same time.

Keep talking and Iran will have nukes real soon, or they will have nuke materials that can be delivered like a dirty bomb. Will they do that? You bet! Not only will they have Nukes soon but, they already have rockets that can hit Israel. They have said, "Israel must be wiped off the face of the earth." Also it is a matter of time, and they will have a rocket that can reach the U.S., with Russia helping them it won't take long. Yes I believe Russia is helping them!

Hopefully we will have enough young, representatives elected to office in this next election. That are Americans for America rather than the people that, will not answer when asked (do you want us to win in Iraqi). We must build up our military strength. Then the rest of the world will see us as strong, rather than weak like they see us now. I feel that we must go all out, for the Reagan star wars defense system. This would make us virtually untouchable. If we do not act now to do this, we are exposing ourselves to these nuts. I feel we must develop the star wars system. That can, sense when a rocket is launched, and be shot down while it is still rising. This way it will pretty much fall back on the sender or close to it. Here is how we should do it. If a peaceful rocket launch is to take place. The country that is launching must give us notice, so we do not shoot it down. Should they do not give us notice we simply shoot it down, 100 % of the time.

Now let's take a look at what would happen, if, the star wars system were in operation. Should North

Korea launch a rocket for testing, we would simply shoot it down. Every time until they went broke or gave up. It is simple! If they cannot test they cannot develop. This would eliminate the delivery capability concerns. It pretty much reads that if we screw around, like the James Baker group wants us to. We are falling into the same trap like we did with Hitler. My question is when will we learn? You cannot pacify a fanatic or a crackpot? No, this will not eliminate, the threat, of a Nuke that can be, delivered by a person carrying it in a suitcase. We will have eliminated the big threat. This will allow us to concentrate more time on securing our borders. What ever we can do to cut down on, the number of threats, will improve security.

I think we have too many Lawyers in Washington rather than real people. The reason I say that is most Lawyers are all mouth, with no substance, or realism at all about situations. They do not create any product, or materially contribute to society, other than, in negative terms. Do not get me wrong, we need some of them to write agreements. But they have gotten out of hand, and we only need about 1/3 of those we have. If you do not believe me look around you, here is what you will see. We have become the sue society! One example is the McDonald's incident, where someone placed a cup of coffee between their legs while driving. It spilled, and the person tried to blame McDonald's because, it was hot! This situation is repeated over, and over daily because, we have too many Lawyers that, have nothing to do. The reason we have most of the problems in Washington, is most of our elected officials are lawyers. The whole point here, where is the common sense that must prevail before acting.

We have gotten way off track, and must get back to the common sense basics, before it is too late. We need to use less words and more action. We need to strengthen our resolve and our defenses so we are strong in every sense. We need to reform the U.N., or get the hell out of it. Or at the very least, pay no more toward the support of it, than any other nation with a vote. Why should we pay more to get our voice heard than any other nation? Let's get real! We are supporting an organization that is a useless, self-serving, money grubbing do-nothing. We are the main supporters of this organization. My question is how *Dumb* can we be? We (the politicians) have tried buying the friendship, of all of the countries that do not agree with us, with the tax money we send Washington. We are getting tired of these self-serving Knuckleheads, thinking this tax money is theirs to, do what they want with it. My question is, are they crazy? Where is their common sense? I really should not ask that question. I know they do not have any. If they did, they would realize that the money is not theirs, to spend like they wish. I would like to be able to handle their family budget for a year. When it was given back to them they would better appreciate, and understand how we feel about what they are doing with our money/resources. I know they would not be happy campers.

They work for us, vote to give themselves a raise. If we are their boss how can they give themselves a raise? Their performance is horrible! They waste most of their time doing nothing, except maybe, exploring how they can spend our money on a useless project. One such example: the bridge in Alaska that will cost $233,000,000.00, for about 50 Eskimos to use for a short period of time, while the ice is unsafe. The bridge has become known, as the bridge to nowhere. Bush asked the representatives to give up their pork barrel projects. Good old Peterson, the Senator from Alaska said "if I have to give up the bridge I will resign." I was waiting for Bush to say sign here, he didn't, and all the others said if he won't we won't either. I lost all respect for Bush! Yes he is our President, but he is not doing the right thing for our country, regarding wasteful spending. I do support him in the fight against the radicals. Again, I ask how *Dumb* can we be? Everyone knows about the $200.00 hammers and the $2,000.00 toilets and all of the other stupid purchases that were made from relatives of our politicians. The part that gets me is do they think we just got off the Turnip truck? That we do not know any better? They think they have to save us from ourselves, in reality it is just the opposite. We need to get them to do something, besides perpetually campaign after they get in, to be reelected to office. Heck they only work about ½ or less of the time they should. Maybe that is a good thing. If they worked like they should, I do not think we could afford the damage they would do. My observation is, we do not have a money problem, we have an idiot (waste) problem, and the politicians are the cause. About 1/3 of our tax dollars are wasted. Yes, about 33 % of our tax dollars are wasted by Washington. This is more than enough to fund Social Security and Medicare. This would also give us enough money to pay down the federal debt. I thought it extremely important to cover this. So you would understand how much of our tax money is wasted.

Reminiscing about my younger years and the good old days! The year is 1940 and I started school. These were tough times TB, Polio, Measles, Yellow fever, Flu, Boils/Carbuncle's, many other illnesses and infections that are not a major problem today were during that time. Like I said earlier, my brother's house was sided with slate siding. That had to have holes drilled in it, to be able to fasten it to the side of the house. I tried to drive a nail in a piece of waste siding and found out why they were drilling holes in it. This is a very vivid thing in my inquiring mind today. It is one of the early experiences that caused me to question everything. Things kind of coasted for me for a couple of years. A youngster was kind of like a car engine, idling, until you grew up enough so you could start to do some work. This lasted until I was about 4 ½ - 5 years old, and inquired why I was not allowed to use a hoe, to weed the rows of vegetables like the older kids were.

This launched my work career. I was assigned several rows of vegetables to keep clean. This was a very important task. We either grew our food or we did not eat. If the weeds were allowed to be near the vegetable plants, they would yield less, and we had less food to eat. All work was inspected every day. If your work was not done you would be sent to bed without being fed. Worse yet you would get extra work for a few days. Spanking was reserved for real bad behavior. You did not want that to happen very often. It was a real atten-

tion getter, I'm 71 years old. I still reach back at my
butt when I think of doing something wrong, and I
only got whipped twice. Welts were about 1/2 inch
high I could not sit comfortably for about 2 weeks,
"spanking works." I know from experience. Today the
kids have it too easy, that is why we have all of the
special ed. Classes, and discipline problems in school.
This is a reflection of the lack of discipline at home,
and in the school. The children of today do not know
the difference between right or wrong. Of course our
wonderful leaders have to tell the parents how to raise
kids, because we are too dumb to know how. "What
a joke." They want us to practice their failed way of
doing things.

Moving on, we made our own toys, out of scraps
of wood, a few nails, and our imagination made them
sound real. The sound effects came naturally because
we knew how a car, a truck or a tractor sounded. We
would make those sounds when we played with the
toys, we made from the wood scraps. We had a big pile
of sand to play on, to get sand only took convincing
our parents, or a neighbor to take the team of horses,
and the wagon to the river. There was all the sand you
wanted for the taking. This same sand was so clean it
was used to make mortar. We spent most of our free
time playing in the sand, with our homemade toys.
We would pretend that we were selling things to each
other, and that we were hauling things from one point
to another to make deliveries.

We would go visit our grandparents about once
or twice a month. They lived about 6 miles from our
house, so we would finish our chores early in the morn-

ing. Then the whole family would walk the 6 miles, visit, have lunch with the grandparents, and walk home so we could do our evening chores. Sometimes our Dad would be home and rested well enough. Then he would hook up old Bob, our horse, to the wagon, and we would not have to walk. This took less time to get to our grandparents house, which gave us more time to visit. This was a real treat, grandma and grandpa had lots of good food, and treats they made. To be sure we were spoiled a little bit. We loved them, and always looked forward to visiting them. My grandparents had an 80 acre farm with about 10 milk cows. All work was done with horses or by hand, the equipment you see today was not even invented yet. With a farm of this size they were busy every day from daylight to dark, milking the cows before daylight, and after dark by hand with kerosene lanterns, the light source.

We had 28 acres of land, 7 acres where we lived and kept our 5 cows, 1 horse and other farm creatures. 21 acres was about 1 mile from the 7 acres, this is where we pastured the cows and one horse. During the summer we would walk the cows and the horse up to the pasture so they could graze for the day. Then in the evening we would walk to the pasture to get them. So we could milk the cows, feed them their grain, and water them. Watering the live stock was not easy like it is today. We had to pump the water by hand into 5 gallon buckets. Carry the buckets about 45 yards to the cattle yard dump the water in the barrel. Repeat the pump, and carry operations until the cattle had all the water they wanted. This was done in the morning before going to school, and in the evening after school along with the other chores.

We must remember this was during the Great Depression. I understand that the kids today do not know anything about the Great Depression or very little. The schools do not teach much about the 1st World War, very little about the 2nd World War, and nothing about the Great Depression, or if they do it is very little. Our kids today do not know about survival. Everything is given to them by their parents or the government through the welfare system. We did not have welfare like we know it today. We all pitched in when there was a problem of any kind. We did not expect, nor could we rely on the government for help. We helped each other. Isn't that a great concept? Wouldn't that be great if we could teach these self-centered kids of today how to be self-reliant, I'm glad I'm passing through this old life during the time I am. The kids of today do not have it easy, because they are not taught to work. Nor do they know where they stand. They have no discipline at home (this is where it starts) or in the schools. The way kids are disciplined today is a joke; it does not get the job done. This is why we have the school shootings and other problems. No one expects the kids to do things, plus the law says, you cannot whip their butt when they do something wrong. There are no consequences for their actions, a result of no discipline.

When I was about 6 my chores increased, to include stacking the wood in the wood shed, to be stored until we needed it. Then in the winter it was my job to fill the wood storage box in the house. This way it was available when needed to heat or cook with. We used wood all year. We cooked, and heated the house with wood. The end of the cook stove had a container that would heat the water for baths or whatever you needed hot water for. During the summer we would go to the river to bathe, it was easier, and you could rinse off really well. Also I was expected to pump some of the water to water the cattle. This chore was very tedious. You worked into it as you grew up. When you could, you got involved in all of the chores, so in case someone got sick you could do their job. The chores had to be done every day with no excuses. The routine was, when you could handle more chores, you were given more to do. There was always more then enough to do, so you were always challenged. There were not enough daylight hours to do all of the chores. You would use a kerosene lantern to finish them, and your school home work. Things were progressing. The equipment to cut hay and put it in the mow, were improving. The only problem was not too many people could afford the equipment. Where it was possible farmers got together, shared the cost and bought a piece of farm equipment. During harvest time they shared the equipment, and helped each other harvest the crops.

The year is 1942. I'm 7 years old we are walking the cows the mile distance to the pasture area. Mother is teaching us German or trying to, because many of the older relatives can't speak English. They are much more comfortable with the native tongue. When we are walking the cows to the pasture there is a "stench" in the air. This stench is the smell of cordite-gun powder, and rotting flesh. We ask how, can that be, the war is far away. Our mother tells us that the air carries the smell great distances. Now that I'm older, and think about it, that makes sense. Unless you experienced it, you would not believe it. The stench was of rotting flesh from the many bodies of the dead from combat. The stench of war is horrible and travels far. I pray that the children of today do not have to endure these things. I had two brothers in the war, one in Europe, and one in the Far East. One was a Frogman and the other an MP. Both got messed up from their combat experiences, with one enduring about 6 months in a Japanese prison camp. He had wounds to his left leg that, that would affect his life permanently, because the wounds were not treated by the Japanese. The other brother served in Europe, and was poisoned by the Germans or French in a village where, he and other American Army personal were enjoying a rest from combat. He almost died, and had many problems for the rest of his life a, result of the poisoning.

As time passed, a result of the need for equipment, required to fight the 2nd World War, the Great Depression was becoming a thing of the past. There were not enough hands to do the work in the factories. This meant the women needed to pitch in, to build the airplanes, tanks, guns, and other equipment, to supply the fighting men on the battle front. The ladies did their part well, and can be proud. It was a time of hardship, and pain for everyone. As a result of the need to make everyone more productive, to supply the war effort, many advances take place in a very short period of time. Many of these advances in technology happened in months rather than years.

It was an interesting time the, progress took many tasks from pitching hay on the wagon by hand. Now hay loaders were invented to pull the hay up on the wagon, and hay forks to put the hay in the mow. There were hay forks that would grab the hay, with a cable winch system to lift it into the barn. The hay still had to be spread in the mow by hand. The first hay balers were becoming available to bale the hay. The first hay balers used a wire tie system to bind the bale. The farmers wanted to get as much hay as they could in a bale. Because the tie wire was expensive, a result the bales weighed 90 to 110 ponds per bale. The bales had to be handled twice, once to place them on the wagon. Then to place them in the barn stacked neatly by hand.

To harvest the grain we used to cut it by hand, bind it in bundles then stack it to cure it. The next progression was a binder that was horse or tractor drawn, that would cut and bind the grain. Now all you had to do is stack it to cure it, until the thrashing rig came to your area. All of the farmers would help each other, to load and feed the thrasher, with a crew to carry the grain up to the bins, where it would be stored until it was needed. Then when needed, all one had to do is open a chute to let it flow into a container, when required for use. Each of these advances made farming less labor intensive. This allowed the farm to be larger, because a person could take care of more acreage. Where grain was grown these advances allowed one person to take care of 2–3 hundred acres or more.

Back in the early 1940s a person was hard pressed to care for 20 - 30 acres.

One must keep in mind that the same advances were taking place in the factories, and on the automobile assembly lines. The electronic equipment and aircraft were greatly improved along with the assembly of them. All things were improving so rapidly it was hard to keep up. We were in the midst of the second Industrial revolution. The U.S.A. was so far ahead of the rest of the world, the great melding pot approach to being free was in motion. Working well, people that came to the U.S.A. to escape oppression in their native land were being innovative, beyond every one's, wildest dreams or imagination. Everything was being powered up. The farmers had tractors available so one person could now take care of 60 acres, rather than 15–20. Grain binders were available to help harvest the grain, choppers to chop up the corn for silage for cattle feed. The farmers had tractors in the 20s and 30s but they were very crude, and no one could afford them until the mid 1940s.

The reason for that is the 2nd World War brought us out of the Great Depression, along with causing the second industrial revolution. The war caused it to take place sooner, rather than later, because of a dire need to be able to supply the war machine. Something the baby boomer generation does not know about, or does not know the truth about. Is what Hitler was doing, while the rest of the world sat back-did nothing. Hitler was gearing up for war, while telling the rest of the world, he wanted peace. In fact Germany was signing peace accords, with any nation they talked to, that they felt was any sort of a threat to them. This was a smart move, on Hitler's part. The, rest of the world was lulled into a false sense of security, and was doing nothing. Hitler actually started his move in 1938. He was removing children from their homes, to be taught what he wanted. Hitler wanted them to learn how to be a good Nazi. Who would do what is asked without questioning it. Actually Germany was responsible for many of the innovations, a result of the war effort. They were developing rockets and machinery of every kind and description. Hitler visualized the need, if he were to be successful, in his endeavor to dominate the World. Near the end of the 2nd World War, Germany was flying Jet fighters. Yes, Germany invented the Jet engine. As said earlier we can thank Hitler's Germany for many of the advancements, we now take for granted. Not that Hitler is to be thanked for anything. He was a tyrant beyond one's wildest imagination; he was obsessed with eliminating all but the Aryan race. He had a screw loose, was crazy! Thank God we were several steps ahead of Germany in most developments. If we had not been the whole world would be a different place today. We would have been dead or doing the German Goose step.

Moving on we will progress through the next years at a rapid rate. So we can get to the real reason for this book like I see it. This industrial revolution did not stop once it was in motion. Instead continued at a rapid pace like an avalanche; there was no stopping it. Looking ahead we saw the harvesting of grain progress to where, the grain is cut, then pulled up an elevator, and thrashed all at the same time. "*The combine*" plus the straw could be chopped, and spread on the fields for mulch. Or it could be discharged in a windrow to be baled for use like mulch. You see this mulch spread on the new seeded areas along side the roads. Corn is no longer cut to be stacked, then shucked, or chopped to be made into silage. Instead the operation is all done in one step, and handled by machinery. Now one person can now take care of 200 to 500 acres of crop land. This progression has taken place throughout every walk of life, and changed everything. This has made the world a smaller place! You can travel to any part of the world in the world in a day or two.

We have spent quite a bit of time talking about Hitler and his devious ways. Hitler was doing his dirty deeds on one side of the world and the Japanese attacked Pearl Harbor on the other side of the world on December 7th 1941. This placed the U.S.A. right in the middle of the 2nd World War. Because both the Germans and the Japanese were talking peace, while preparing for war, we were not prepared. Because we, just like the rest of the world wanted to believe, beyond all hope. That everything will be Ok, if we just did what they wanted. After all they were talking about peace. How easy we are deceived! Thank God we were running ahead, of both of these tyrants in the progress field. We developed the Atomic bomb just months, ahead of Germany, and Japan. Both had a big head start. The great melding pot called America, with its mix of people that wanted freedom won that one.

We have moved very quickly out of the labor intensive farming and industrial area, into the advanced automated society we have today. This has made us more productive with less effort. This part of it is good but for every action there is a reaction. The reaction to the tough times has been "I do not want my children to have to work hard like I had to, to make a living." A result of this, it has become too easy for our children of today, to get what they want. Most of them are spoiled. If you do not believe me just watch the smaller children when you are in a store, and they are in the same store with their parents. Mom and Dad cannot afford what they want, or do not want them to have it. I will tell a true story about when, in the Wal-Mart store in Ava, Missouri. This young Momma had her 3 year old with her. He wanted some candy, Momma said no. This brat started pinching Momma's face and screaming. I said to Momma when she was going out of the store, take him behind the cars. Whip his little butt this way he will understand, what he is doing does not get him, what he wants. The next thing I see is her arm going up, and down on his bared butt, right where it should be. As we walked by the little boy is crying. He is saying "Momma I'm sorry, I love you Momma" and hugging his Momma. When we walk by she says, "thank you that sure works good." I tell her practice it, and you will have a good boy. The problem with making it too easy is where do you stop? We are way beyond that point it is so easy for the kids today, that most are, creeps. There is no consequence for their actions. Let us look at why this has taken place, other than the parents wanting to make it easier for them.

We have our good old greedy, self-serving, ego

maniac, know it all elected officials. They cannot handle their job or their families, and think they know how to raise kids. They say you cannot spank your kid's little butts. Take a look at what is being said here, I will use an example to make my point. Would you want a boy like the Kennedy, he was caught in the middle of the night drunk, on dope, and ran his car into another. He claims immunity because he is a Congressman. He starts making excuses for what he has done, than his old man gets it covered up for him. By the way his old man is a Senator, one of the Pork kings, and may be the top Pork king. There are no consequences for his actions, and this is not the first time he has done this. You must remember he is one of the self-serving idiots, we are talking about. He is one of our fearless leaders, no wonder we have problems in Washington. God, save us, these Knuckleheads will not. We have the likes of Al Gore the green man, who does not practice what he preaches. And Ted the socialist dry drunk, with the dry drunk part being questionable.

Hey, all the jerks are not men we, have those with a skirt, that think they know what is best. Such as Barbara Boxer, and the likes of Feinstein, Hilary Rodham Clinton or is it Hillary Clinton? Speaking of Hillary, I asked an older lady, if she would consider voting for Hillary. She looked at me in disgust, and shook her head no, than said she would, make an exception to that. She said, "If Hillary would commit to Divorce that idiot, she is married to if elected, I would consider voting for her because, if she did that, I would know she had a brain." I have talked to many women, and have only one say they would vote for

Hillary. They said the reason they would not vote for her is the "Clintons are not trustworthy people." Then we have the medical guru, sue happy, Lawyer Edwards. Who knows it all, and changes like the wind, this is dictated by, what is expedient or best for the moment. Then we have Randy "Duke" Cunningham who, was caught, and convicted for corruption, Nov. 2006, is serving an 8 year prison sentence. Now listen to this: he receives a $64,000.00 a year pension. That's right he receives a reward, paid for by our tax dollars for being a crook, a convicted felon.

We have them from both sides of the isle. Here are the names of a few: former Minn. Sen. David Durenberger, former New York Rep. John Murphy, Kentucky Rep. Carroll Hubbard, former New York Rep. Mario Biaggi and many more. They are all convicted felons that either are in prison or have served prison time. The worse one is Dan Rostenkowski, the former Congressman from Illinois. He did about all the crooked things you can imagine. He was indicted in 1994 plead guilty to mail fraud, and was convicted. He served only 15 months in prison. He still receives an estimated $126,000.00 a year pension. Congress has done nothing to stop this, I feel it is because they are all crooks, and if caught they want to receive a pension also. They are not interested in doing the right thing for America. Instead they are only interested in doing what serves them best. Washington is full of trash. I do not know how long the U.S.A. can continue to survive what they are doing to us.

One must realize that we are presented with what the political machine wants us to have to vote for.

So we get those individuals that will best serve the Democrats or the Republicans, not what is best for the country. Their thinking is the party above all else, at all costs, to hell with the U.S. A. So we vote for the lesser of two evils. We do not have an offering of an American for America we never have an offering, a person that will do what is right. The political machine only presents us, with what they want from both of the crooked parties. Now let us add the rest of the trash to the bucket, Hollywood and the ACLU. It just does not get any worse than this. Except maybe Washington vies for the label quite often. They just do not want to be out done when it comes to titles.

At one time the ACLU was a good organization. That served a real purpose that time has long passed. They are now a liberal organization that, stands in the way of any good. To see what is being said here all one needs to do, is go watch a movie. You will see that most of the movie content expounds trash. This is shown in the way of sexually explicit acts, or violent acts that are so gory, it is beyond belief. T.V. is not much better. The ACLU protects this kind of trash. They say it is free speech. So now tell me why? Would we wonder where our kids get the crazy ideas from, to do some of the things that they do at home or in the schools. Hell, the things they see every day teach them it. Most of our kids today spend, way too—-much time watching TV or doing nothing, there is no one asking them to do something. So they come up with their own ideas, based on what they are exposed to. Most of their waking hours are spent in front of the tube. Our kids are too mobile, have too little to do. In too many cases there is not a man in the household. There is no consequence for their actions. So what do we expect? We are getting a return proportional to the effort we put into them.

Enter the law, and we add another screwed up idea, it says you cannot spank them, should not holler at them. Time out is OK for little kids 5, and younger, it does not make an impression on older kids. They think it is a joke, in order for it to work, a parent has to be there to enforce it. Most parents today are too busy, or too lazy, to take the time required for time out to be effective. If you question what is being said here, all you need to do is sit on a bench at your nearest Wal-Mart store. Observe the behavior, and butts of the people waddling by. Now you will see, and hear the answer if you listen to what is said. We do have a small percentage of the overweight people that do, have health problems and regardless of what they do, they will have weight problems. God bless you, we do not mean to offend you, and we love you. The rest of you did not get that way by being active. To raise kids requires you to be real active in their lives. Watching TV and eating are not activities that will help your kids or your butt. In defense of those parents that do work, and work at doing a good job. Single and married do, not be offended by what is being said here. Let your conscience be your guide, you know who you are. If you do not, just look in a mirror, be honest, and you will find out. Now let's talk about another system run amuck.

Now we need to talk about our good old top heavy school system that has one agenda. Get more money to spend to accomplish less. The schools are government run this, is controlled like welfare. The government doles out the money, to them this, requires a layer or two of paper work to justify everything. The better job that is done with the paper work telling, the system what they want to hear, the more money the school gets. Like it was said in a school board meeting, I an interested Grandfather-tax payer attended. The school board explained we have this new found money that we can get from the state. If we can get the local sales tax increase passed. I asked why are you saying, new found money? All of the money comes from us. I made a point of the fact that if we approve the tax at the local level. Then the school gets more money from the state, which they did not get before. If all of the schools in the state get this "new found money" then the state must increase the tax. To meet the need, and on and on it goes, where it stops nobody knows. Talk about a screwed up system. I told them we must pay off our credit cards. How in the hell can you say new found money. Because we the people do not provide open end credit cards to the local, state or federal governments.

They act like they found the money alongside the road, and it is free, if you wonder why we have a problem with the school system, think about it no longer. The scenario we just talked about, should give you an insight into why, we have the problem. Can you imagine a child being raised in a home with no discipline, then going to school to be taught, by teachers that think things are free? Do they think that there is no end to what they can spend? Do they think the kids are stupid? That they do not pick up on what they do? Maybe, just maybe the kids are smarter than they are, and can see what is taking place. Because these people that are teaching our kids do, these dumb things, the kids think that it is the way to do things. After all these people (our teachers are educated, therefore smart, right) don't really have common sense. These people were taught by the same failed system that does not demand performance; they are a puppet of their teachers. So what do you expect? In defense of the good teachers that do exist. And there are quite a few, these words are not meant for you. Unfortunately you are a minority! Keep up the good work if, the system will allow you to. We thank you for what you do. For the rest of you, you should be flipping hamburgers. You would maybe do a good job of it if, you had a good teacher. You are parrots, and can only do what you are shown, just as you did in college.

Parrots are not what we need for teachers. Parrots cannot adjust to changing circumstances and with a room full of children circumstances change by the minute. At least things will change until you, the person in charge, a teacher, establish what the ground rules are, so the kids know where they stand. Once you let the kids know what is, and is not acceptable. They will feel secure when they know you are fair in your dealings with them. They can trust you because, you say what you mean, are reasonable, use common sense. You will follow up on everything instantly. The follow-up part is so important along with the follow-up being done quickly. The attention span is not too long for the younger children. Do it quick and with love, because they can sense how you feel about them. They will react according to how they feel. Teaching is a tough job and a teacher that can do the job well, has a God given talent that is a valuable asset. Just like our children are gifts from God. Now I know some of you will be offended by the God part. Then I say so be it. Our currency says "In God we trust" and when we stop trusting in God, and following his commandments, we will fail. Look at the situation! We sure cannot trust our government to do things right, and we sure cannot trust big money to do things right. We sure as hell cannot trust that, perverted group in Hollywood to do anything that is good for the country. All we have is God, and if we place our trust in him. Follow his commandments we will be a strong well rounded country with good moral, ethical, and sound basis for existing. We have drifted so far off of this path. Unless we return to it we will soon fail as a nation.

If you ask why say these things about what, is happening to out great country. We feel you may be part of the problem because, you are part of this me society we have become, that has evolved through time, and is the problem. Just in case you do not understand what the, me society is. We will explain so you know. The, me society consists of people that are self-centered, self-serving, egotistical, what makes me feel good, immoral, unethical, undisciplined, perverted minority-majority? These people use credit irresponsibly have road rage when they do not get their way. Do not discipline themselves, or their children, and will not stop to help a person in trouble. Instead will look the other way making, believe they did not see what was happening. Can you imagine a society that is made up of a majority of people that think this way? We in the U.S.A. are split about 50–50 at this time. If you do not believe what is being said here, look around, and you will see everything I speak of. The Judges turn perverts loose to kill someone, sometimes in a matter of weeks after being turned loose.

The credit thing is way out of control—- our children think sex, drugs and other bad actions are o.k. Because that is what they see most of on TV (thank you Hollywood for displaying your perverted thinking on TV and thank you our stupid leaders for allowing it to happen; you are perverted also). How on God's earth can we expect our kids to behave responsibly if we do not? But instead show them the trash they see daily on TV, and see on the news what our elected officials do that is immoral. The government passes laws that say do, not spank your kids (but they want you to be responsible and want to hold you responsible for what your kids do). The kids play that idea like a Banjo especially, when they become teenagers (the age of rebellion). They know that if you whip their butt, all they need to do is complain to a teacher, and you get in trouble with the law. Now here comes the interesting part of this: if you spank their butt or smack them to shut up their rebellious mouth. Some idiot will be sent to your house that has no children, and was taught by a failing system, about how to handle things. He-she does not give a damn about what happened, to cause the problem. So it becomes a real big mess, because this person does not have enough common sense, to come in out of the rain, let alone get involved in a family situation.

Now I do not condone child abuse, the child abusers must be caught up with. What I'm talking about is rational, common sense discipline, being applied to a disobedient child, that may have snuck out to drink, have sex, steal or God only knows what else. Can you imagine some idiot telling you to give a teenager time out? With our failed system, all the teen needs to do is complain, and the idiot will be back with reinforcements. I sure hope you can see the fallacy of this. Maybe you have had the unpleasant experience, I'm talking about here. I sure hope not! To give you an example of how teenagers use what is said to avoid doing the right thing. This morning 4/13/2007, I took two teenage girls to school, and when I went to pick them up I looked at the house. It was dusty, dirty, and just generally a mess. So we talked about it. All the girls kept saying it is not our job, Mom makes the rules, and it's Mom's job. I told them that cleanliness is everyone's job, get the house clean, and don't make excuses. I'm not interested in your excuses. The only reason a house is dirty is you are lazy. When I was a kid, dirt in the house was not tolerated. My mother told us if it is on the floor pick it up, regardless of whom it belongs to. Our house will be neat at all times, if it is out of place it is your job, each and every one.

You will contribute at all times, no excuses. The grandkids got lippy with me, so I told them that when I was a kid growing up, you did not talk back or you would have a fat lip, at the very least. If it did not stop instantly, you got your butt busted in a way that you would remember for a long time. So stop the excuses, I'm not interested in them. Just get the job done and shut up. It is everyone's job to keep the things picked up and the house clean. My how things have changed to an atmosphere that created good, obedient children to one that creates creeps. We have a bumper crop of them today. If you don't believe me just look around, many of the kids today are fat, mouthy, and lazy. Not all, just most of you and you know who you are. The rest of you do not be offended.

The only way this can be straightened out is to get back to basics. It used to be reading, writing and arithmetic, and a consequence for your actions proportional to the offense. Time out is ok for small children, 2 to 5 years old if it is supervised. A smack on the butt goes a long ways toward making good kids. The discipline must be immediate when the children are young. Their attention span is short if, it isn't done immediately they will not know what it is for. After they reach about 3 years old they know, when they have done something wrong, than discipline can be administered. Whenever they are caught up with: they will know what it is for. I'm old fashioned, and believe in "Spare the rod and spoil the child." We sure have come a long way from doing what works to what does not. In defense of my grandchildren they are really good kids for the most part. But a kid will test you at every turn. If you fail the test they will follow up with further testing to see how far they can go. This testing is how they learn by trial and error, in the event they do something wrong it must be corrected immediately. If you have young children expect to be tested often. Enjoy!

We need to get our heads out of the sand and pay attention to what works and what does not. Let us take this thinking a step further. Apply it to the lessons taught us by the actions of Germany, Japan, Italy, and all other groups that talk peace. While preparing for war because they believe that their way is the only way. They need to dominate the world in order to make it perfect according to their thinking. Hitler was preaching peace, signing peace accords with other nations. When he got started he would sign a peace accord then invade the same country within a short period of time. Ditto for the Japanese and Italians as the whole bunch were in cahoots with one another. Germany and Japan had the plans in place on how they would divide the world up. Germany would control Europe and Japan, the Asian portion of the populace. Having read the first part of the book you will have a good grasp of the history of the things that lead up to the 2nd World War. How everyone was deceived because they wanted peace at all costs. Rather than face the truth. Like the Ostrich they buried their heads in the sand.

So what's new here? Now we have another faction that is doing the same thing and the world is burying their head in the sand again, by ignoring what is taking place. We have most of the non-Muslim nations saying "oh, let's talk to them if Iran gets the nuclear bomb, it will be ok." Just remember not a single Muslim faction has denounced the actions of the radicals. They refuse to answer when asked "do you condemn what the Radicals are doing?" This really takes the cake! We have a person running for President of the U.S.A. Barack Hussein Obama who was raised a Muslim. This is hearsay and I do not know if it is true: This information was-is available on the Internet. When Obama was sworn in as the U.S. senator from Illinois he used the Koran not the Bible? He will not honor the pledge to our flag? He will not put his hand over his heart when our national anthem is played? God save us if he is elected President. Can we take a chance on these things being true? The President of the U.S.A. must be a person that not only is capable of running the country, that person must also be above reproach. This person will have enough to do, and cannot be distracted by their past, like Clinton was.

We cannot trust Russia with the present leadership. We cannot turn our back on China. Germany is not to be relied on, France is not a friend although we saved their butts twice, at a great cost of American lives. Mexico is so corrupt that even with all the oil wealth, the people are destitute, and want to escape to the U.S.A. Some of South America is rapidly going socialistic. Most of the rest of the world is in turmoil. We do have Australia, England, Canada, Japan, and I'm not sure how many other nations beyond that are with us. I believe that Russia and China are supplying weapons to the radical Muslims, so they can get them to do their dirty work. If you look you will see that Russia and China are supplying Iran, Iran using those supplies to supply the Radicals in Iraq, and elsewhere. If you think these two are our friends, I say we don't need enemies. We cannot talk the radicals into doing what we want. While we talk they are using the time to get more weapons. Or nuclear weapons so they can blow our butts up like the 9/11 attack but 1000 times greater. The only solution is to close our borders, get a handle on who comes, and goes in the U.S.A. and build up our military strength. There is peace in strength and unity because unless we start to pull together we will all hang separately. "United we stand, divided we fall."

We need to stop the welfare programs, both the national and international welfare, we cannot buy peace. Peace is like respect. You earn it by being strong and diligent. So let's start doing both right now. Unless the countries that we give vast amounts of our tax dollars to join us, to do the right thing, let's get some sense, and shut off the giveaway programs. Ever since Russia has come under the leadership, of the former KGB officer, Russia has reverted back to the old ways. Freedom is stifled, you cannot tell the truth, if the Russian government does not agree, with what you have to say. Or if you do say something, the Russian government does not want you to say, and you push the issue, you die of a mysterious poisoning of some sort. In China you have the freedom to do what the government wants you to do. But like Russia if you push the issue you have serious health problems, or are arrested for speaking your thoughts. These are typical examples of the sort of governments our leaders give our tax dollars-support to. They use the money to build up their war machinery whether we like it or not. They allow trade with these goons, this in an attempt to buy peace, instead of getting peace in return, we are digging a deeper hole for our next generation by creating more debt. The piper must be paid at some time. The balance of trade, pork barrel projects, welfare, stealing and other foolish spending is out of control. Needless to say the federal credit card has limits just like ours does. Stop the waste! Now!

The only people that do not think so are the fools in Washington. They use our tax dollars to try to make them selves look good. My question for them is why do they not do the honest thing, for the betterment of the U.S.A? Rather than the self-serving thing they do. Freedom of speech and freedom of expression are good. But when you disrespect people and National beliefs then you should be deported. Because you live in or are visiting America you must assimilate. We are expected to when we travel to an Arab country. Women are required to wear head covering. No alcohol beverages are allowed. Why then do we accept that an Arab can come to America, and not have to follow our traditions? Plus they get offended when, they have to obey our laws. Will use our freedom of speech against us every chance they get, if they do not like what we do, why don't they go back where they came from? We should not change for them they must change for us, follow our traditions and laws or get out of the U.S.A.

America is a great country. But is being ruined by the pacifists that think, we can talk our way out of having to do the right things. Take a look around you if you open your eyes, you will see most people are enjoying the easy life. They have new cars, new houses, all the toys, "A chicken in every pot and a Volkswagen in every driveway." Their kids have everything they whine for. That is how most of the kids get what they, want Mom and Dad take the easy road. In defense of the good Moms and Dads you know who you are. Your kids behave when you go to the store, or out to dinner so relax, this is not meant for you. Keep up the good work this is, what life is all about. You can be proud of your kids, and yourselves.

We just had the worst shooting spree take place at, a college in Virginia on 4/16/2007. The person doing the shooting was mentally ill, it was known he was. The judge allowed him to decide if he wanted help. He bought a pistol at a gun store in Virginia, never should have happened, a person who is mentally ill is not allowed to purchase a gun. This would not have happened, if it was reported that he had a mental condition. He slipped through the cracks because he was allowed to decide if he wanted, help with his mental condition. Now we have the gun ban idiots all over this, because they are so dense. They believe that a gun is the problem. To find out if what they are saying is true do this: take a gun, load it, lay it on the ground, and see if it tries to shoot someone. A gun is simply a piece of steel. Unless a person picks it up to shoot it, it will just lay there and rust, just like any other piece of steel. Now let us look at another piece of steel, about one inch square by 24 inches long. We lay it on the ground, and it just lays there, all it will do is rust just like the other piece of steel, called a gun. The only difference is the shape. Now some person that wants to harm another comes along, picks up the piece of steel, and beats someone to death.

Do we ban all steel of various dimensions, because a person with mental problems of whatever sort can, use them to kill another person? Let's take this a step further a person uses a car to run another person down, killing them. Do we ban cars? A knife is used, do we ban knives? A baseball bat is used now, what do we do? I will quit here because I think you get the point, so we will go forward. The point of this talk is simply to point out that we have a very serious problem, with where the fault lies. All of these inanimate objects are harmless, until they are made mobile by a human being. *HMMM* I guess we have to work on the thing that is really the fault, or cause of this problem rather than blame an inanimate object. The point being Stable people, do not kill other people. So we the majority who are Stable, must give in to a few troubled people again? I for one just cannot believe that kind of thinking. The majority of us are supporting, too many of these troubled-lazy people as it is. If we give in to that thinking pretty soon more people will be troubled-lazy. Somewhere-somehow common sense must prevail!

Why do I say that? Because people are just naturally lazy and many are troubled, it may be easier then facing life for them. People are lazy that is natural, and normal that's why we invent things to allow more work to be done, with less effort. We still need the hands on people to do the field work, to harvest many of the vegetables for our tables. So this means there are jobs, for all that want to, or will work? If you do not believe this, just take a look at all of the illegal aliens that we have in the U.S.A. they are working. When we do the right thing, and get them out of our country, the able bodied welfare people can do the work. This will provide jobs for everyone. No it does not pay top dollar, the skill level required is not too great it just takes effort. We have a group of welfare recipients that could do these jobs, except for one problem: they are too lazy to help themselves. We have made them slaves of the government, by not expecting them to help themselves. We have made them fat and lazy. People on welfare do not appreciate what they get, for the most part, because it is too easy.

So we need to cut off some of the help so they get thin and hungry. Then they will accept these jobs, and work, this will make them feel good about themselves. This will be good for them and America. If this is done there will be four loud noises emitting from the same sources, that make noises whenever there is a threat of taking away some of the welfare. All are liberal, we will call them Al, Jesse, National Argumentative Association Causing Problems and Dem. You know who they are. They will say affirmative action is a must because we have been down trodden for years. I say to them "*Oh Bull,* travel on your merit or don't go." Too many of them that are on welfare, have kids with no Daddies present in the household. They generally feel sorry for themselves. The self pity thing has been worn out, let's stop making excuses, and get with the program. You should not be given preferential treatment because you are lazy. The problem can only be solved when your leaders stop preaching that, you deserve to be supported by someone else. Yes your leaders are to blame, for much if not all of your problems. No one owes you a damn thing so stop whining. You say we do not respect you, and you are right, respect is earned not given. You do not earn it by someone else supporting you, and feeding the kids you fathered.

Just so you understand where I'm coming from I will tell a true story about raising 5 boys. One boy had a black friend, another boy a Mexican friend, we had 7 horses (all kids like horses) Benny and Jose would be invited to spend the weekend, just like all the other boy's friends. Most times there were 6 to 20 kids at our house on weekends during the summer. All kids were told the rules, they had to obey, and the consequences if they did not. Everyone behaved well. One of our animals was a Jackass, named Jack, was easy going except you had to announce yourself, or he would kick the crap out of you. To him it did not matter if you were black, white, or brown. There were several other Black and Mexican kids that were friends of the boys also. I tell this story only so you can understand how I feel about color, I'm like Jack. Good kids are good kids just as good people are good people; we both are color blind. Most of the Black and Mexican kids were being raised on welfare. It was a real treat for them to get out of the environment they were living in, spend time out in the country, they enjoyed it, and behaved well. We also insisted that we meet the parents, to let them see, what their kids were doing when at our house. Some had it real rough but all were good people. Several of our boys stayed at their friend's house on weekends, some of the houses were in areas where you did not go out at night. The parents told us not to worry because they do not go out, and the kids will not be allowed to either. We really enjoyed having the kids and their parents over at our house. They all were good people simply victims of circumstances beyond their control. Regardless of color or origin we are all Americans, and we better start acting like we are, or our problems will get worse if we don't.

I have seen the changes in our legal system through the years, and what has happened is not good. In the good old days, if you broke the law you paid for it, like the law said you would. Today there are too many law breakers that literally, get by with, murder. The whole legal system in the U.S.A. has gone wacky. Let's start with the speed limits on our highways, when the posted limit is 55 MPH. It should mean 55 + 3 to 4 MPH. When I travel I have had to go as fast as 80 to 90 MPH just to keep up, to a semi-truck, or car in many cases. The reason I went that fast is to find out how fast they were going, because they passed me so quickly. So why bother to post a speed limit if it does not mean what it says? Let us keep it simple. Why post a speed limit at all, if it does not mean anything? By doing what is happening with the speed limit, we make the law meaningless. From here it gets worse most laws are handled about the same, like the speed limits, with plea bargaining, and buying your way out of trouble in many cases. This lack of a consequence to suit the disobedience of the law makes the law a joke. A good example of what is being said is the young Kennedy incident he used his position as a congressman to get off the hook when he was caught drunk and driving. Now we go to the next step with the more serious cases. Where judges are turning sexual predator-pedophiles loose only to have them pursue, and kill women or children in many cases within weeks of release. I feel that a judge that turns one of these predators loose should, serve the time or pay the consequences for the crime that the predator did. My question: are these judges that turn these sexual predators-pedophiles loose, sick individuals themselves?

Thank God there are not too many of these judges that are of this ilk. We must get rid of those that are to protect our children. The legal system has problems that go way beyond this it, does nothing to protect us from the illegal aliens that enter the U.S.A. Take for instance a drug dealer who has been caught by our border patrol on numerous occasions, is deported-repeats the offense several times is, shot in the butt by the border patrol. Then he is given immunity so, he can testify against the border patrol Deputies that shot him. Get this! During the time after the illegal alien was given immunity from prosecution, he is caught with 750 pounds of drugs. This is his third offense, and he is still allowed to testify against the border patrol. Plus his testimony is believed, and the border patrol Deputies are convicted. This in itself is really bad news, let alone the fact that the individuals are placed in prison, and are exposed to illegal alien drug dealers in that prison, rather than in a protected environment. Guess what happens? They get beat up really bad, and the woman that is the warden at that prison, makes excuses for her actions. If you watch the news you see this sort of thing happening daily, with no real consequences that are comparable to the offenses.

Now let us look at how the news media handles

these stories: most of the media will downplay the facts instead of blame something other than the thing or person at fault. For instance if someone is shot, they blame the gun rather than the person that pulled the trigger. I ask have you ever seen a gun go around pulling its own trigger. Come on a gun is a piece of steel, an inanimate object that is made of steel, and capable of rusting is all. Where is the common sense? Thank God for Fox news and Bill O'Reilly. Bill tells it like it is with generous amounts of common sense applied. Bill has started several movements that removed a number of these sick judges. What really stands out with Bill is he follows up so something happens. Keep up the good work, Bill. We applaud you and support your efforts.

If the rest of the news stations such as NBC, ABC and the others would report and support the truth. We could pressure the do-nothing representatives in Washington to move, so the penalty would fit the crimes. I feel a sexual predator should be castrated at the very least for the first offense. If they do any other crimes, then put them in prison for life, so they cannot ruin anymore young lives, or kill anymore people. Again, thank God for Bill O' Reilly because if it were not for him exposing the liberal wacko judges. The sexual predators would still be turned loose our laws still do not impose a penalty proportional to the crime, but it's a good start. There must be a severe enough consequence for their actions, so they have second thoughts. Plea bargaining should not be an option in most cases, the law states what the penalty must be. So judges must enforce the law, not make law from the bench: just do your job, you are paid to do. Judges you also swore on a bible that you would uphold the law, what's to misunderstand here?

Minorities have more clout than we, the majority because our legal system, judges, and our supposed leaders, cater to them. Why do they cater to the minorities? They cater to them because if they do not Jesse Jackson, and several others will make them uncomfortable. Lets face it they do this to get the minority vote, plain and simple. They take the easy way, rather than the right way, because it takes less effort, and feel if they cater to them everything will be ok. No it will not be ok unless we do something to make it ok. The inaction of our leaders in Washington will not solve the problems. No more than allowing the pork barrel spending to continue will help lessen our national debt. Action creates solutions, not talk. Yes you must talk about how to solve a problem. But not forever, because procrastination is not a solution, even though the people in Washington think so. Let's look at a particular situation, where a minority group is getting their way. The illegal alien people that jump our border bring dope to our country, and our legal system finds them more believable than our border guards.

Take a look at another group that is having babies out of wedlock, with no daddies present to support the kids, and the mom is on welfare. These groups get preferential treatment. They are supported with our tax dollars, are lazy, and have no intentions of trying to find a job. If you give them a job most of them will not show up for work much of the time. Plus if they do show up they will steal from you. Our Washington group is using our tax dollars to support these people, using our tax money to buy votes. Now again I will defend those that are not as described. I know some that need help that are really good people, and feel the same way I do, about this situation. We must help you that are sincere and really need it.

Now let us look at how we think we can buy friends around the world. I support helping those that really need it, but our leaders have a real problem in determining who needs help and who doesn't. So they seem to give every country help, with no contingencies, in most cases it ends up wasting our tax dollars with much of the money stolen. I do not know where they get off, thinking if we throw a dollar blanket over a problem, it will go away. You would think they would have gotten the picture by now, but they just keep trying the same sick tricks. In case they still haven't gotten it, by the time this reaches print, do this. If what you are doing does not work, then you must change something. I have watched a Monkey try to do something, and when they were having a problem, they tried different things, until they found a way that worked. Now I'm not saying a Monkey is smarter than our leaders, you draw your own conclusions about that.

We have said many things here, but the main thrust of this diatribe, is to point out the similarities of past, and present circumstances. How we as a country along with the rest of the pacifist people of the world. Are reacting to what is happening, just like happened, before the 2nd World War. These events are so similar you could remove the faces of the people talking peace. Compare the context with Hitler's, and you would hardly be able to recognize any difference. Just listen: "Our Nuclear activity is for peaceful purposes," "We have joined the nuclear club," "the, demonstration was illegal." Note these people were protesting their country reverting back to an iron-fisted way of rule. One of the other countries that, enjoys favored trade status, is using the money to build a large war machine. They keep their people destitute, and we cater to them. So I ask of you, what are we, and the rest of the world doing different than was done before the 2nd World War? Everyone says talk to them. We and the rest of the world talked to them before the 2nd World War for 10–15 years, and they were building up their war machine. They used talk as a stalling tactic, lulling the world into a sense of false security, saying everything will be ok, they are peaceful. Then when Hitler started invading countries in Europe we still ignored what was happening.

In the meantime Japan was building a robust war machine and we ignored all of the things that were happening, until Japan bombed Pearl Harbor. Now we finally woke up to reality. We were not strong because we wanted to believe that the actions of Germany, and Japan would not affect us. So we tried to stay out of the war until our hand was forced. The lesson of that should be that, we are hopeful of peace. But prepared for the worst, and in my opinion we better get with the program, we are not prepared. The next world war will be devastating to the whole world, If not the end of civilization as we know it will come to an end. Any country that is not prepared ahead of time will be beat before they get started, the war will last for weeks, at most, a result of technology. We know we cannot fight a land war with most of the countries, they have overwhelming numbers. So it will be a nuclear war, once it starts. Otherwise we do not stand a chance. What it amounts to, is we will be damned if we do, and damned if we don't. If we are strong, the chances of a war not being started are better strength is the best way to deter a potential enemy, from doing something foolish because the consequences will be too great.

There are so many factors in place that contribute to my conclusions. Such as the radical Muslims that have a scorched earth agenda. They are pursuing what reads as follows. If you do not agree with us you must be killed. "Israel must be wiped off the face of the earth" and everyone but those that believe like we do are of the devil. These are their beliefs, and if we talk to them we can convince them they are ok, we are ok. The let's live in peace group worldwide are sucking their thumbs. Just as they did when Hitler was signing peace accords, and talking peace with countries in Europe. Then Hitler was invading their country within weeks or months of the signing of the accords. We have various agreements with some of these countries at this time, and have had for a number of years. They have not done, and are not doing what they agreed to in the past. So what value does another piece of paper have? Like the Chinese say America is the paper Tiger, they say this because we have relied on a piece of paper (an agreement to solve problems for us). A piece of paper is no better than the honor of the signatories. In the past about 60% or more have not honored what they have signed on to.

Not a good track record that you can take to the bank. It is like a bounced check, which in turn if you deposit it, and write checks based on it being good causes you trouble. I have studied the ways of the Middle East for many years. They have been warring with each other forever, the whole area is made up of tribes, with various beliefs, and they would fight whenever their paths crossed. The only time they join together is, when the enemy of my enemy is hated worse than my enemy. Then they would join forces to beat the enemy, when the enemy was beaten they would resume fighting amongst themselves. That is where we are at in Iraq we are the enemy of my enemy. I think that Iran said it best, "we hate the Iraqi's for what they have done but we hate the American's more." One must remember one thing about these people: if you kill my brother, I'm duty bound to get revenge. Then that family is duty bound to get revenge, this thinking is perpetual, it just does not stop. Pretty soon the whole group is duty bound to get revenge, on one another. Guess what. We have killed many of these people, enough that if you follow their thinking. They just cannot get enough of us they need a Nuke to be able to catch up. Now if you think this statement is not correct just look around. They have many people that will strap on explosives, and blow themselves up to get revenge.

They just do not have enough explosives or enough people, to get the revenge they are duty bound to get, with the methods they are using. They need a better method to get the job done. They will not give up easily that you can see by what is happening in Afghanistan, Iraqi and other parts of the world.

Now that we know what we are dealing with, what are you our elected leaders going to do? I sure hope that your way of solving the problem, is not like it has been. All you have been doing is talking-debating-bickering, with no action. Inaction will not get the job done inaction, or the kind of action that has been advocated to date is playing into the radical Muslims hands. We have Harry Reid ready to call it quits he says we have lost the war. I'm sure glad he was not in charge at the time of the 2nd World War we all would have been doing Hitler's Goose step. Isn't he just the kind of leader that makes you proud to be an American? Oh we have more. Take Teddy from Massachusetts or Jefferson who likes cold cash, and Peterson who likes bridges that serve no purpose. What does he care the bridge only costs $233,000,000.00 or with the over-runs that are typical, maybe closer to $500,000,000.00. Who knows how much more? Listen to this! He was honored for his 47 years of service. I did not know that we honored people for serving themselves. He loves pork.

Oh we cannot forget bomb, bomb, bomb Iran Mc Cain, I believe he is a disguised Democrat, he and Teddy are buddy's. He has to be a real winner! He cannot keep his foot out of his mouth, just like good old Reid or Murtha. He and Reid are a trip as they both think about the same way. Then we have the person that thinks she is the President of the U.S.A. Good old Nancy Pelosi who thinks she can run the U.S.A.

from her position as majority speaker. She should be tried for treason she is betraying us with her actions. Because she is majority speaker gives no right to try to speak for our government. Like the people from other countries say. Just leave America alone they will destroy themselves from within. As "united we stand, and divided we fall." With all the bickering, and divisiveness of the Presidential debates it makes one wonder how much the people running for President hate each other. Than we have Hollywood trying to run, or ruin the county along with the fools that talk, talk, talk. Disagree, and bicker with no unity whatsoever you wonder who the enemy is? Then we have our good friends from other countries that we believe are providing weapons to the radicals, and cheering them on, because now they have someone to do their dirty work. If you do not know who they are, one is the reason we had a cold war, and the other is using our markets to play us like a fiddle. We have the beer drinkers, and the wine makers that live close to each other. We saved one's butt during the Second World War, and the other was the reason we fought the Second World War in Europe.

I do not like war anymore than you do but 9/11 did happen. We did have to respond to the enemy that did use our airplanes as weapons, and killed about 3000 of our people. Just remember Pearl Harbor like you do the Alamo, do not forget 9/11 and get back at the foe. I believe Bush did the right thing in Afghanistan, and in Iraqi. I just believe he screwed up after the fact, by not responding with an overwhelming force. If you enter a war you must overwhelm the enemy to win.

I did not like Rummy to start with, I thought he was an arrogant Knucklehead that was insecure in what he was doing, and was on an ego trip. We needed a person with a good head which he did not have. Now enter the liberal media that spends 90% of their air time repeating negative news to badmouth our President. I feel that during a time of war that should be looked upon like treason. In a time of war we must support the troops that are in harm's way. We must be united and support our president, the majority elected him. The conservatives would support a liberal if elected we supported Clinton when he was president. We did not like Clinton because of what he did, but he was our President, and elected by the majority so he was supported by all of us Americans. We must remember that whatever is said is available, to the whole world in a matter of seconds on TV. The media must be held accountable, shouldn't they?

Yes we have free speech, and that is why the troops are fighting. So the media can have the freedom to say, whatever is on their mind. But I believe that if they cannot report the good along with the bad, then they must shut up. What happened to accentuate the positive, or telling the truth? To tell the truth means you tell both sides of a story, not just one side. Fox news comes as close as you can get to being fair and balanced. They report both sides of the story. Bill O' Reilly does a good job of researching things before he talks. Unlike some of the other TV news channels that report lies, wait until people have them stuck in their proverbial craw, before they even attempt to correct their error. I question if Dan's statements were an error, or a propaganda maneuver to discredit our President. You decide, enough of those misstatements have taken place, that the possibility; of it being done on purpose exists. I believe it was done on purpose, after it was on the news people said, "did you hear what Bush has done now" Dan knew this would happen. The harm has been done, and the correction may not even reach the rest of the world. If it does it may not register, in many cases it did not in the U.S.A. A liberal is a liberal, and does not want to believe any good of another person unless they agree with their agenda, and they have one. Most of them would not believe a person that disagrees with them, if it is the truth they believe what Hollywood and the liberal media speak is the only truth even if it is a lie. There are many in Hollywood, think they know how to run things here in the U.S.A. better than the President.

If you want to know the truth about Hollywood all you have to do is watch several of the movies they produce. In almost every one of them you will see a complete lack of moral values. They use vulgar language, violence and sex to sell their wares. No wonder our kids have problems! They spend more time watching TV than any other activity. If you watched what they watch constantly you would have your thinking saturated with morbid thinking also. In defense of the few people that do create good clean movies. You know who you are, do not take offense. We are talking about the shoot 'em up, bang 'em up and beat 'em up violent movies with a scattering of sex that dominate the movie scene. If you had this trash constantly in front of you during your formative years, you would think that it is the way of life, what do we expect? Then we have the likes of George Soros who is trying to buy the Presidency of the U.S.A with, the large amounts of cash he makes with his offshore companies. That pay little or no tax to the U.S.A. and I will bet that he did not serve in the service of the U.S. military to, protect the right to speak like he pleases. Then we cannot forget the strange one Rosie, she is a trip, with her big mouth, and what she jabbers about. Hollywood is full of people like this we have to protect our kids from them as Washington will not. Also we have that moveon.org group that tells stories without checking them out, and most of them turn out to be untrue.

My purpose was to give you an overview of what we are faced with: an overview of the 1st and 2nd World Wars. How little we have learned from those experiences and the similarities of those times, and where we are today. If we do not strengthen our military, join hands for the common good, and stay strong in our resolve to overcome the problems that face us as a country. The outcome may very well be much different than what it was during the 2nd World War. Yes we are at war! The war is not well-defined because the enemy does not expose himself like they did in the past. There are not any well-defined borders to this war. Instead the enemy is evasive they look like, walk, and talk like the rest of the population. Because they are part of the population except their mentality is morbid. They will strap explosives on their body then mix with the rest of the populace, and blow themselves up in the midst of good people. Where are their borders? They are in every country in the world this makes it everyone's problem, except most of the world does not want to believe that is the case. They believe that if we treat them well they will not bother us.

We treated Hitler and the Japanese well. That did not stop them but instead gave them an indication we were weak. They continued their advances until it was almost too late. The Oceans will not protect us like they did during the 2nd World War. Technology has shortened the time to reach any part of the world to hours rather than weeks or months. This radical group that is scattered all over the world has beliefs you cannot fathom. Because you and I will not blow ourselves up in the name of Allah, God or whatever name they may use. These people will, they crave a Nuke so they can be even more devastating. When they get a Nuke they will use it. We must gather together like one to stop them or pay a horrendous price for our stupidity. We cannot rely on help from most of the rest of the world at this time. It appears that many of them want to see us destroyed because they envy what we have, and do not know how to get it. Yet! In fact most of the rest of the countries that have the wherewithal to help the radicals are doing just that. They are supplying weapons to the radicals to be used against our troops in Afghanistan and Iraq an attempt to embarrass us with defeat. Plus we have the likes of Reid, Murtha, Pelosi and others in the U.S. they are willing to help them by accepting defeat. In my humble opinion defeat is not an option. Because that will give the radicals more resolve to fight harder. Now that we know that we are being led down the same path. Like we were before the 2nd World War by the radicals around the world, and that some of our supposed allies are helping them.

We must be united with a strong military as a deterrent so our enemies are not tempted to attack us. This is the single most important action we can take. All other things are a mute point if we cannot defend ourselves. Or we do not have enough strength so no one like a single country or as a group will try to attack us. We must be secure above all else. Be supportive of our president, do not be a back stabber like many of you have been. You know who you are, and you should be ashamed of yourselves. The whole world knows you just like I do, so shame on you. We must back our President even if we do not like him the majority elected him so support him because, if we do not we demonstrate to the rest of the world that the great experiment, America, is failing. We are not failing we are in a period of adjustment.

Once we have security in place at least to a point where it is not a distraction. Then we can concentrate on the other problems that confront us. The legal system needs to be reformed. It is a joke! Like it is today we have judges that make law from the bench rather than enforce the laws of the land. This must stop. To do this will require that many judges get let go, or prosecuted for contempt of the law, for not following the law as written. If the law as written does not do the job required of it. Then our legislators must rectify the problem quickly, not in their normal bicker-debate for years until they get the law to suit their purpose. But instead get good laws in place for the good of the country. The politicians must not be exempt from obeying the law. The law of the land applies to all in the land, including those that are allowed here on visas or any other reason: no one is exempt.

When we go visit another country we must assimilate, i.e. when Nancy Pelosi went to the Arab countries she had to cover her head, to satisfy the Muslim traditions. She also had to obey their laws. Why then do we not require that the Muslims assimilate when they come to our country? I for one do not understand this double standard. We follow their traditions when we go to their country, and we must obey their laws. Then when they come to our country they must follow our traditions, and obey our laws. I just do not understand why we cater to them this way. Let us take another example: in the Detroit, Michigan suburb of Dearborn, the Muslims are allowed to disobey our noise ordinance laws, to make loud announcements. They say is a call to prayer, and do it 5 times a day. Let us take a look at the double standard here: we cannot practice Christianity in most of the Muslim countries. Let alone make loud noises to announce a call to prayer. Why do we allow them to disturb the peace in our country? I'm not saying they should not be allowed to practice their beliefs, simply that we have laws everyone else must obey, why not them? When they come to our country we cater to them, when we go to their country they make us conform to their ways. I just do not get it! This type of catering to them is exactly what happened before the 2nd World War. If they do not like America well enough to assimilate, send them back to where they came from. Before we go on there is one other thing I feel we need to address. It is a question. How many of the Muslims that are in our country have denounced the Radical Muslim attacks, on us and our troops? I think this should be enough to tell us why we must not change for them. But if they want to stay in our country they must assimilate or get out.

Next we must do something different than we do now, about what Hollywood can put on the screen. If what they do in the name of free speech is causing our kids to believe something that is bad news. Then I say it is no longer free speech. Take a look! Almost everything that hits the theater or the T.V. screen has sexual content, and violence like shooting, killing, beating, and foul language. Is this what we want our kids to learn? That sick group in Hollywood must be controlled if we are to get a handle on what our kids think is right or wrong. 90% of what they see on the screens is bad news. Can you imagine growing up seeing this trash most of your waking hours, during your formative years? Now you think that is the way of life, it is not what we want, or need if, we want good kids, and grownups in our society. This is exactly what the Muslims do, to indoctrinate their kids to get them to believe that strapping on a belt loaded with explosives is ok, in the name of Allah. If you wonder why we have the problems in the schools with the shootings, all you need to do is watch what is on T.V. and you will see the reason. If you don't see the reasoning here then you are a part of why we have the problem. Most Hollywood movies are violent shoot 'em up sex action type movies. With the kids spending more time in front of the tube they are taught by Hollywood, how to do the shoot 'em up, things they act out on a regular basis. I know if you watch the news at least once a week you, will see a reenactment of a Hollywood movie on the news. Like one of their bang 'em up, shoot 'em up movie presentations. Where else are the kids taught these demented things?

So now that we know what the problems are. We ask our politicians, what are you going to do? Procrastination, debate, and bickering will not solve the problem, positive action will. You people work for us, spend only about ½ the time you should at work, and when you are there you do nothing. Plus you get benefits that are the envy of the rest of the world your, perks are something else. I cannot imagine a company in the world that could exist, if their employees received perks like you people do. Plus you get, all you can finagle with your power brokering activities, and the crooked lobbying payola that takes place. When you do get caught you are the only group that I know of, that police yourselves. You have passed laws that only seem to pertain to us. You cover up for each other when caught doing something wrong, you feel you are above the law; i.e. the cold cash that was found in the freezer or the young Kennedy thing. This is crazy, who can believe you? Most of you are self-serving crooks. Think about it for one minute. If I were to do what you do I would not have a job. I'm expected be on the job, do something productive while I'm there, or they fire me. Why should you be treated any different?

Yes, America is the greatest nation on earth. With freedoms that are the envy of the rest of the world, and most of you politicians are working your butts off to try to destroy us. Why? Are you that greedy? Are you that self-serving? Don't you believe in our system of governing? Don't you believe people should be free? It appears to me that you do not want America to be strong. Because most of you care about Pork projects more than you do about balancing the budget. You just don't seem to give a damn about anyone, or anything but yourself. You spend our tax dollars foolishly you, bicker-debate, and just don't get the job done. So where is your value? I truly believe you, and the likes of you want the U.S.A. to fail. You are dragging the greatest country in the world, America down with your lack of resolve when it comes to solving our nation's problems. I watch the news, and the polls say that your approval rating is 18%. From where I stand with talking to people I believe it is closer to 5% at least that is what I get. I think the difference is your polls are run in a liberal area, and the poll I run was in a mixed area. In any case you are not worth the damn. "Let us not ask what we can get from our country, but what we can give to keep our country great." Let us use common sense when governing, instead of trying to throw more money at everything let's be prudent. Look at how what you do will affect the U.S.A. that must be # 1. As it is all that happens in Washington is tax and spend and spend and tax. It is time to get serious about what is done with our resources.

Here is what a person born September 6th 1935 believes has happened to America. We have wandered off the path of greatness with our liberal ways. Most of you think we can spend our way out of trouble. Hard work has gone to the wayside. We are raising kids that are over indulged, we live on credit we are self-serving for the most part. We do not give a damn about our fellow man. We are departing from what our founding fathers based our whole system on, a belief in the blessings God has bestowed on us and the freedoms to self govern. When we turn our back on God, He will turn his back on us, and we will surely fail. We cannot let a few tell most of us what is right or wrong because if we do like we have done we will have a big mess. This has been happening, and must change it must be the majority rules. We cannot have a judge, or a few judges tell the majority of us that we do not know what is good for us. This has happened too often. They serve us, not we, them, let's ask them to serve, or get out of the way, and the same goes for you, our elected officials. Then we have San Francisco, one of the prettiest cities in the U.S. with more deviates with distorted values than you can imagine. I have seen the U.S.A. go from a good, moral country, with a superior work ethic. Where most people were prudent, and responsible with money, and resources where a lady acted like a lady. Not like a gaudy woman that provides oral sex, or grabs at a man's privates, like some of the girls of today do. In fact it is not uncommon for the boys to get what the girls call a head job, at school. Or on the school bus, we have teachers having sex with their students. In fact it seems there is an epidemic of this activity. Ever since Bill Clinton did the Monica thing the kids seem to think oral sex is not sex. Bill Clinton said "I did not have sex with that woman" we can thank Bill Clinton for causing our kids to believe that a head job (oral sex) is not sex. We could go on about this kind of discussion for quite some time but enough of that.

So I ask now that we know all of these things that we have seen, and experienced living in the greatest country in the world. What are we going to do to change things so we can once again, make America the greatest nation the world has ever seen? It is not a question of whether we need to change our ways. It is a question of how to change them, for if we keep on doing what we are doing we are destined to fail. Most of the rest of the world is doing all they can to expedite the process. We are helping them with our wanting the good life without earning it. The following statement expresses exactly how I feel about catering to any person that wants to become an American citizen. This says it all! The year is 1907, our President is Roosevelt and he has this to say about immigrants. There are many arriving everyday with 5,000 or more arriving at Ellis Island some days. The year is 1907 but the speaker knew what he was talking about. Here are Theodore Roosevelt's ideas on immigrants and being an American in 1907.

"In the first place, we should insist that if the immigrant who comes here in good faith becomes an American and assimilates himself to us, he shall be treated on an exact equality with everyone else, for it is an outrage to discriminate against any such man because of creed or birthplace or origin. But this is predicated upon the person's becoming in every facet an American, and nothing but an American. But something else also isn't an American at all. We have room for but one flag, the American flag. We have room for but one language here and that is the English language and we have room for but one sole loyalty and that is a loyalty to the American people." Theodore Roosevelt 1907

Let them come but they must assimilate, this is America. We are a nation of Christians. Our language is English and they must learn English and obey our laws. This is how our President felt about immigrants then and I feel we should not change, they must learn English. The tests to become a citizen of the U.S.A. must be in English, if we start to cater to them we will have clans in areas that cannot and will not learn English. This has been and is happening so now we adjust to their thinking? No, because if we go to their country we must obey their laws and follow their customs. If you want an example take a look at Pelosi wearing a head cover when she went to the Arab countries. We should require they remove their head cover when they come to our country. The answer is simple: assimilate, assimilate, assimilate or leave. I wonder what part of this they do not understand. I was raised and grew up in the greatest country in the world. I for one wish for the great experiment, America, to remain the greatest country in the world so in closing I say God bless America, we love you.

In his inaugural address on January 20th, 1961 President Kennedy spoke eloquently of America's role in the world community. "Let every nation know whether it wishes us well or ill that we shall pay any price, bear any burden, meet any hardship, support any friend, oppose any foe, in order to assure the survival and success of liberty."

We need to spend time talking about 9/11 so we do not forget what the radicals will do if we let our guard down. Remember what they did and prepare ourselves with good security. So they cannot do it again because sure as you read this they are trying to find a weak spot, so they can hit us again. With North Korea and Iran plus some other elements in the world wanting our demise, the next one may be a Nuke. We like President Reagan's way of looking at how to handle a war cold or otherwise. We Americans have a short memory and this is a lesson that I sure hope we do not forget. If we do, the next one may not be easy like 9/11 was, for everyday that goes by the radicals are one day closer to having a dirty bomb or worse, a nuke, so remember this lesson long and well.

You don't realize how much you miss Ronald Reagan until you read and remember some of the stuff he said and stood for. The following quotes are what he used during the debates when he was running for president and after he was in office, they sure ring true today.

"Here's my strategy on the Cold War: We win they lose."

"The most terrifying words in the English language are: I'm from the government and I'm here to help you."

"The trouble with our liberal friends is not that they're ignorant: It's just that they know so much that isn't so."

"Of the four wars in my lifetime none came about because the U.S. was too strong."

"I have wondered at times about what the Ten

Commandments would have looked like if Moses had run them through the U.S. Congress."

"The taxpayer: That's someone who works for the government but doesn't have to take the civil service examination."

"The nearest thing to eternal life we will ever see is a government program."

"I've laid down the law, though to everyone from now on about anything that happens: no matter what time it is Wake me, even if it's in the middle of a cabinet meeting."

"It has been said that politics is the second oldest profession. I have learned that it bears a striking resemblance to the first."

"Government's view of the economy could be summed up in a few phrases: If it moves, tax it. If it keeps moving, regulate it. And if it stops moving, subsidize it."

"Politics is not a bad profession. If you succeed there are many rewards, if you disgrace yourself you can always write a book."

"No arsenal or no weapon in the arsenals of the world is as formidable like the will and moral courage of free men and women."

"If we ever forget we're one nation under God, then we will be a nation gone under."

The next subject is the gasoline shortage. A lot of folks can't understand how we came to have an oil shortage in our country. Well there's a very simple answer.

"Nobody bothered to check the oil."

"We just did not know we were getting low."

"The reason for that is purely geographical."

"Our oil is located in Alaska, California, Coastal Florida, Coastal Louisiana, Kansas, Oklahoma, Pennsylvania and Texas." Our DIPSTICKS are located in Washington, DC" any questions?

In closing remember we have several enemies; one is waste 1/3 of our tax dollars disappear down a black hole when arriving in Washington. If the waste is stopped it will provide enough money. To fund social security, Medicare and pay down the federal debt without tax increases from now on. The other enemy is our elected officials for not doing the right things for America.

Now that we know what is wrong with America, my question to you is. What are you as an individual going to do to help make it right? Basically it is real simple: "United we stand, divided we fall" so I say to you Brown, White, Yellow or Black, we must all be Americans first then of German, Oriental, Polish, African or whatever descent. Above all we must be Americans first so we have a united front. This way our enemies cannot misunderstand what we as a nation will do if we must defend our freedoms. God bless all of you. God bless America and those in the world that stand with us to defend freedom. Best regards, Ken Hoffman